Foreword

Making your own pillows is an ideal way to add color, interest and drama to your home.

Included in this book are ideas for decorator pillows, quick and easy projects, gifts for loved ones, and pillows incorporating vintage fabrics and trims.

Choose a pillow to match your own skill level and see how easy and satisfying it is to create your own decorator accents.

Table of contents

Decorator Style

Interior designers use pillows to "pull a room together". You can follow their lead by adding that decorative touch at a fraction of the cost! Novelty buttons, exquisite trims, lush fabric textures, upholstery samples are all components of one-of-a-kind pillows designed to enhance decor. Experiment, and let your imagination guide your interior design creativity!

Faux Leopard
(page 5)

You will need:
1 18" pillow form
3/4 yd. green brocade fabric
1/2 yd. leopard print fabric
1/2 yd. coordinating leopard print fabric
2 1/2 yds. moss green ribbon trim - 2 1/8" wide
1 1/2" yds. black satin ruffle ribbon - 1" wide
2 yds. black bullion fringe - 3" wide
Scraps of both leopard prints for buttons
4 - 1 1/2" button forms
1 - 2 3/8" button forms

1. CUT FABRIC: Cut one leopard print (A) 10"x10" and the other (B) 14"x14". Cut green brocade 19"x19" for front piece and two 13" x 19" pieces for back.

2. DECORATE: Sew 10" leopard square (A) in center of 14" leopard square (B). Sew on green trim, mitering corners and covering raw edges. Sew this to the center of the 19"x19" green brocade piece.

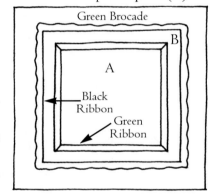

Sew on black trim, also mitering corners.

3. BACK: On wrong side of the two 13"x19" pieces, turn in a 1/2" hem on the long ends, press. Turn in another 1/2", press, pin and machine stitch close to edge. Remove pins. With right side facing up and hemmed edges on the inside, overlap the two back pieces by 5" so that they create one 19"x19" piece. Pin together along hemmed edges and set aside.

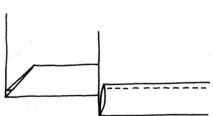

FRINGE: Matching bound edge of fringe with raw edge of green brocade fabric front piece, machine baste fringe to right side. Overlap ends of fringe 1/2".

SEW FRONT TO BACK: Pin the front to the back, right sides together. Sew a 1/2" seam allowance all around. Trim corners, remove pins and insert pillow form.

4. ADD BUTTONS AND DECORATIONS: Fold four pieces of the green trim as shown (A) and tack together. Then put the four pieces together to form a medallion as shown (B). Tack to pillow as shown in photo. Cover four 1 1/4"button forms with one of the leopard prints, following manufacturer's instructions. Cover 2 1/4" button with the other leopard print. Sew the small buttons to each corner of the black trim. Sew the large button to the middle of the medallion.

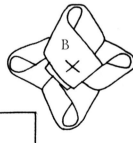

Faux Leopard Pair

Exotic faux animal prints--shades of Theda Bara, and the 20s--add dramatic interest in this grouping of large and small pillows. Two corresponding fabric prints, a band of gold brocade, fringes, ribbons, and covered buttons add decadence. The premade bolster was then trimmed to match with a band of animal print tied with tassels.

Toile Cameo
(page 7)

You will need
18" pillow form
3/4 yd. black velvet or velveteen
1/2 yd. leopard print fabric
1/4 yd. black and white toile print
Small amount of cotton batting
1 1/2 yds. black satin gimp - 1" wide
2 1/2 yds. zig zag cord - 1/2" wide
1 yd. black satin ruffle ribbon - 1" wide
2 1/2 yds. black and white cord trim - 1/2" wide
4 black silk tassels
4 - 4" black and white ornate tassels

1. CUT FABRIC: Cut one piece black velvet 19"x19" for front and two pieces 13"x19" for back. Cut leopard fabric 13"x13". Cut black and white toile using oval pattern on p. 121.

2. DECORATE: Top-stitch toile oval to leopard print leaving small opening at bottom of oval. Stuff cotton batting in oval through this opening. Hand stitch closed.

3. Sew length of zig zag cord around toile oval, beginning and ending at bottom of oval.

4. Center leopard square on square of black velvet and sew in place. Sew black gimp trim to edge of leopard square. Set aside.

5. BACK: On wrong side of the two 13"x19" pieces, turn in a 1/2" hem on the long ends, press. Turn in another 1/2", press, pin and machine stitch close to edge. Remove pins. With right side facing up and hemmed edges on the inside, overlap the two back pieces by 5" so that they create one 19"x19" piece. Pin together along hemmed edges and set aside.

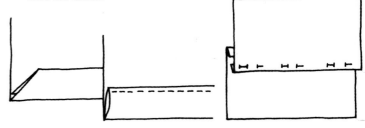

6. FRINGE: Matching bound edge of fringe with raw edge of black fabric front piece, machine baste fringe to right side. Overlap ends of fringe 1/2".

7. SEW FRONT TO BACK: Pin the front to the back, right sides together. Sew a 1/2" seam allowance all around. Trim corners, remove pins, turn right side out. Insert pillow form.

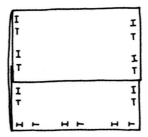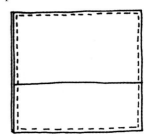

8. Hand stitch a black tassel to each corner of pillow.

9. With black ruffled ribbon, stitch eight loops of varying lengths to bottom center of toile oval.

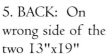

10. Sew one black and white tassel securely to each corner of pillow.

11. Cut 4 - 6" and 1 - 10" lengths of remaining zig zag cord. Wind each length in a circular direction and glue to create "buttons". Sew the largest to the bottom of the oval. Sew remaining 4 "buttons" to corners of pillow to cover where black and white tassels are attached.

Toile Cameo

Dramatic black and white set the tone for this sophisticated pillow accent grouping. Black toile print depicts a familial scene in the center. Surrounded by a black trim and leopard print frame fastened by a rosette, the design forms a bold focal point against the solid black background. Black and white trim and tassels, accent this knife-edge pillow.

Toile Flange Pillow
(page 9)

You will need:
16" pillow form
3/4 yds. white candlewick fabric
1/2 yd. red toile fabric
1 1/2 yds. red gimp trim - 3/8" wide

1. CUT FABRIC: Cut the white fabric 21"x47".
Cut red toile 11"x11".

2. DECORATE: Sew the toile square to center of
the right side of fabric. Sew the gimp trim around
the edge of toile fabric.

3. ASSEMBLE: On wrong side of fabric at each
short end, turn in a 1/4" hem. Press. Turn in
another 1/2", press, pin and machine stitch close
to edge. Remove pins.

4. Fold fabric in half widthwise, right sides
together. Measure 10" on either side of this fold.

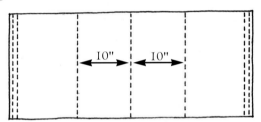

Fold at this point (at each
end) and press. The fabric
will overlap in the middle.
Sew up each raw edge with
1/2" seam allowance.

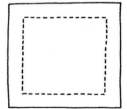

5. Turn right side out. Trim
corners. Top stitch all
around, 2 1/2" from the
edge. Insert pillow form.

Red Toile Envelope Pillow
(page 9)

You will need:
14" pillow form
1/2 yd. floral fabric
1/4 yd. red/beige gingham
Toile fabric scrap
3 flat button covers - 1 5/8"
3 beige tassels
24" burgundy gimp trim

1. CUT FABRIC: Cut two 15"x15" squares of
floral fabric. Cut two 6 1/2"x14 1/2" pieces of
gingham for flap.

2. ASSEMBLE: Pin gingham pieces right sides
together. Sew 1/2" seams around three sides leaving one long side open. Press open seams. Turn
right side out and press again.

3. Place and pin flap at top of a floral square,
right sides together (A). Place other floral square
right side down on top of this (B). Stitch, with
1/2" seam, leaving opening at bottom. Trim corners, turn right side out and press.

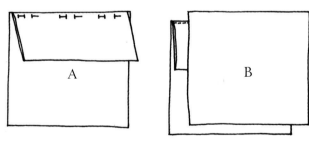

4. Insert pillow form and hand stitch closed.
Cover buttons with red toile fabric following manufacturer's instructions and sew to pillow flap.

5. Tie a tassel to each button. Glue red trim
around pillow flap.

Red Toile Envelope Pillow and Toile Flange

A work of art in itself, a softly muted vintage floral fabric serves as the body of this elegant envelope pillow. A coordinating red checked fabric flap, bordered in red trim highlights the covered buttons and tassels. Buttons are covered in scraps of red toile fabric used in the matching flange pillow. This pillow was made using a candlewick type fabric, embellished with a lovely toile scene.

Gathered Tapestry Roses
(p. 11)

You will need:
14" pillow form
1/2 yd. tapestry fabric
15" tapestry trim (to match fabric)
1 yd. braided cord
2 yds. bullion fringe - 3" wide

1. CUT FABRIC: Cut fabric 15"x24" for front and and two 11"x15" pieces for back.

2. FRONT: On 15"x24" piece, sew gathering stitch (with strong thread) 1/2" from top and bottom edge and 5" from top and bottom edge.

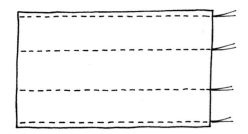

Pull up these gathers to 15" and secure.

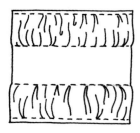

3. Sew tapestry trim at center and sew braided cord over each edge.

4. Matching bound edge of fringe with raw edge of fabric, machine baste fringe to right side of gathered fabric. Overlap ends of fringe 1/2". Use masking tape to hold fringe out of way.

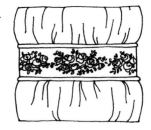

5. BACK: On wrong side of the two 11"x15" pieces, turn in a 1/2" hem on the long ends, press.

Turn in another 1/2", press, pin and machine stitch close to edge. Remove pins. With right side facing up and hemmed edges on the inside, overlap the two back pieces by 5" so that they create one 15"x15" piece. Pin together along hemmed edges.

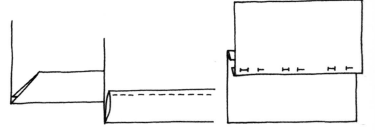

6. SEWING FRONT TO BACK: (Note: Use zipper foot to sew pillow.) Pin the front to the back, right sides together. Sew a 1/2" seam allowance all around. Remove pins. Remove masking tape. Turn inside out and insert pillow form.

Tip -
For a fuller, fluffier pillow, try using a floral chintz fabric for this project. Accessorize the pillow with a contrasting bad of striped fabric for a cozy English cottage look.

Gathered Tapestry Roses

Antique tapestry fabric in a watercolor floral softly gathered and pouffed makes a richly adorned companion in this grouping. Lovely Victorian ribbon centers the pillow and heavy bullion fringe all around finishes this luxurious feminine pillow.

Golden Medallions
(page 13)

You will need:
14" pillow form
1/2 yd. gold brocade fabric
2 1/4 yd. gold cord - 3/8" wide
2 tassels - 3"
1 1/3 yds. gathered gold ribbon
1 decorative button

1. CUT FABRIC: Cut gold brocade fabric 15"x15" for front and 2 pieces 11"x15" for back.

2. BACK: On wrong side of the two 11"x15" pieces, turn in a 1/2" hem on the long ends, press. Turn in another 1/2", press, pin and machine stitch close to edge. Remove pins. With right side facing up and hemmed edges on the inside, overlap the two back pieces by 5" so that they create one 15"x15" piece. Pin together along hemmed edges and set aside.

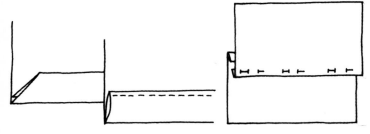

3. TO MAKE THE WELTING: Cut gold brocade fabric on the bias to make three 3"x20" strips. Sew together into 60" strip (see welting instructions p. 104). Press seams open. Fold in half wrong sides together, sandwiching welting. Pin and sew close to welting with zipper foot.

4. Pin and sew welting around pillow front so that edge of cord is 1/2" from pillow edge. Where the welting ends meet, tuck the raw edge inside the overlap. Stitch across joint.

5. SEW FRONT TO BACK: Sew pillow front to pillow back, right sides together. Trim corners, turn right side out and insert pillow form.

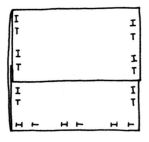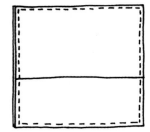

6. DECORATE: Cut a piece of cord 80" long and tie around pillow as if wrapping a gift, cinching pillow tightly.

7. Tie cord in a knot. Tie each end in a knot, and glue tassels to ends.

8. Cut one gold ribbon 18" long and another 25". Form these into circles, one slightly larger than the other. Overlap ends and tack.

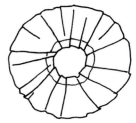

9. Glue the smaller circle inside the larger one.

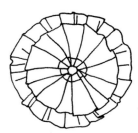

Glue the decorative button to the middle of the smaller circle. Tack this piece where cords intercept.

Golden Medallion

Make this elegant brocade welt-edge pillow from glowing, gold fabric, or choose a color to compliment your room.   Add a two-tone silk cord, with deeply-fringed tassels, and a luxurious metallic ribbon rosette, anchored by a gold button. This classy decorator pillow is perfect for a contemporary setting, or to add a final rich touch of belle epoque!

Silk Floral

White silk, soft and glowing forms the backdrop for a patch of cream silk peonies. Surrounded by a trim of satin posies, this elegant creation can become the centerpiece of a grouping of embroidered bed pillows, or recline with rich brocade pouffes on a chaise lounge. Tres chic!

Ethereal Pockets

Ethereal and provocative, the translucent images are almost dreamlike. Easily change this silken pillow with your moods. Slip mementos, and seasonal fragments of nature into four little sheer organza pockets caught by narrow cream lace trim, and centered on a white silk brocade background.

Silk Floral
(page 14)

You will need:
16" pillow form
Premade silk pillow - from (Arty's #SCC-44)
9 silk flowers - 3"
1 yd. floral trim

1. Hand sew or glue floral trim 3" in from edge of pillow, forming an 8" square.

2. Tack the flowers on one at a time filling in the square.

3. Unzip the pillow and insert pillow form.

Ethereal Pockets
(page 15)

You will need:
16" pillow form
Premade silk pillow - from (Arty's #SCC-44)
1 1/2 yds. white flat trim - 3/16" wide
1/4 yd. white organza
Iron-on hem tape (optional)
Fabric glue

1. CUT FABRIC: Cut organza into two pieces - 9 1/2" x 5 1/4" each.

2. Fold under 1/4" on all sides and press. Baste or fuse hems.

3. Pin to pillow top as shown. Hand sew or iron in position on sides and bottoms of pockets. Then sew down middle.

4. Glue or hand stitch flat trim over this seam.

5. Slip in mementos or decorative objects such as - old photos, leaves, flat shells, feathers, silk flowers, antique scraps of lace, antique envelopes with calligraphy.

Tip -
Other ideas for decorating silk pillows:

Floral pillow - Use large, colorful pom poms to fill the square, contrasted with a matching trim, or use a variety of silk flowers within the square.

Pocket pillow - change the character of the Ethereal Pockets by adding your own touches. Create a decorator statement by enclosing fern fronds in each pocket and display near a framed fern.

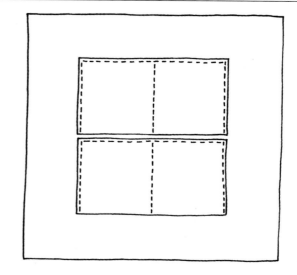

Fresh Country Style

Ah, the country! For each person the word evokes a different origin, yet they are all images of comfort, simplicity, and uncomplicated style. American, English, French, Scandinavian--country furnishings and eclectic blends fill rooms in modern apartments, suburban houses, and rural cottages, all right at home! Even in the most "modern" setting, a country pillow adds a nostalgic touch of comfort.

Ruffled Gingham and Morning Glories

Equally at home against embroidered white bed linens or in a grouping on a white wicker settee, Morning Glories climb all over this colorful chintz pillow. Two rows of complimentary trim pick up the hues in the blossoms, and act as a border for the deep, gathered blue gingham checked ruffle.

Blue and white looks good anywhere. Especially restful in a bedroom, this grouping combines ruffled toile covered pillows, with sheer lace for a clean, fresh setting. Find toile fabric to match the wall covering pattern, or a different pattern in the same color. When they're grouped, the effect will be the same. Sprigged floral and crisp stripes add to the beautiful blend.

Ruffled Gingham and Morning Glories
(page 19)

You will need:
12" pillow form
1 yd. blue gingham fabric
1/2 yd. floral fabric
1 1/2 yds. ecru cord trim
1 1/2 yds. pink twisted cord trim
Fabric glue

1. CUT FABRIC: Cut floral fabric 13"x13" for front piece and two pieces 10"x13" for pillow backs.

2. RUFFLE: Cut 3 pieces of gingham fabric for ruffle 12"x45". 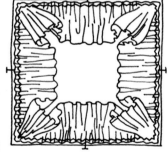 With right sides together, sew short ends using 1/2" seams to make one long strip. Sew ends to make one continuous loop. Press seams open. Fold loop in half lengthwise, with right sides out, and press fold. Fold loop in quarters and mark divisions with pins or small marks in seam allowance. Make two rows of gathering stitches, one along seam line and the other just within seam allowance. Gather ruffle to match pillow. With pins, mark midpoints along edges of pillow top. Match to quarter marks on ruffle loop. With right sides together and raw edges aligned, pin ruffle to pillow top. Distribute gathers evenly, allowing a little extra at corners. Pin or tape ruffle away from edges and machine baste around edge using 1/2" seam allowance and pivoting at corners.

3. BACK: On wrong side of the two 10"x13" pieces, turn in a 1/2" hem on the long ends, press. Turn in another 1/2", press, pin and machine stitch close to edge. Remove pins. With right side facing up and hemmed edges on the inside, overlap the two back pieces by 5" so that they create one 13"x13" piece. Pin together along hemmed edges.

4. SEW FRONT TO BACK: Pin the front to the back, right sides together. Sew a 1/2" seam allowance all around. Trim corners and remove pins. Turn right side out.

5. Glue ecru cord around edge of pillow top and then glue pink cord right above that. Trim ends to match exactly and neaten with glue. Insert pillow form.

French Provençal with Covered buttons
(page 21)

You will need:
12" pillow form
1/2 yd. floral fabric
1/4 yd. pink/white ticking
1 1/2 yds. blue rickrack
8 - 1 1/8" button forms
Fabric glue

1. CUT FABRIC: Cut a 13" square of floral fabric for front piece. Cut two 10"x13" floral pieces for pillow backs. Cut four 4"x13" strips of ticking fabric.

2. FRONT: Sew front ticking strips to center floral square, right sides together with a 1/2" seam. Press seams open.

3. BACK: On wrong side of the two 10"x13" pieces, turn in a 1/2" hem on the long ends, press. Turn in another 1/2", press, pin and machine stitch close to edge. Remove pins. With right side facing up and hemmed edges on the inside, overlap the two back pieces by 5" so that they create one 13"x13" piece. Pin together along hemmed edges. Sew the ticking panels to this back piece. Press seams open.

4. SEW FRONT TO BACK: Pin front to back (right sides together) and sew together with 1/2" seams. Trim corners, turn right side out, and insert pillow form. Pin along ticking panels and "stitch in the ditch". Glue rickrack around pillow, over seams. Cover buttons (following manufacturer's instructions) using scraps of the floral fabric. Sew buttons to ticking panels (as pictured).

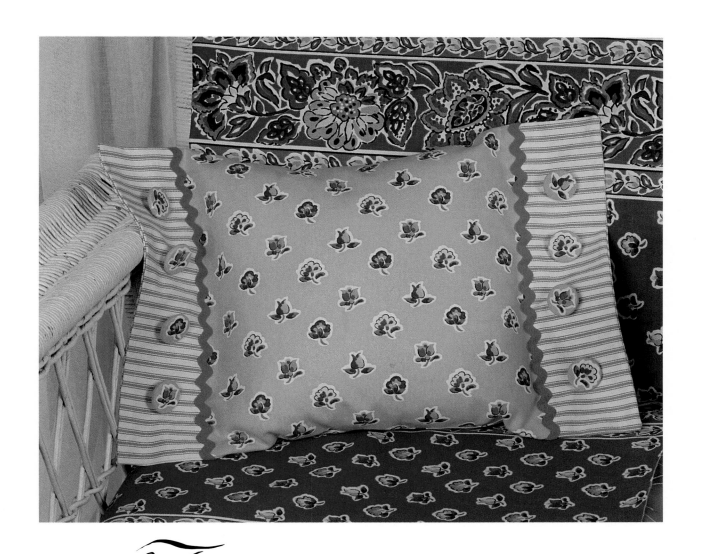

French Provençal with Covered Buttons

Sunny French provençal print with contrasting pink and white ticking borders this casual pillow, and picks up the fabric color on the wicker settee. Wide, blue rickrack pull the two elements together. Round buttons, covered in the same butter yellow material, add a designer touch. C'est la vie!

Bow-Tied Country

Red checked gingham peeks out of a textured floral envelope cover on this easy-to-make pillow. Green plaid ties keep envelope secure. For a wintry look, substitute cranberry velvet for the gingham.

Scotty

This tartan accent is so "dog-gone" easy! Two squares of bright tartan fabric tied on top of a simple black and white gingham checked pillow start you off. Applique a smart little Scotty dog with a yellow bow in the center, then wrap it up with red ribbons.

Bow-Tied Country

(page 22)

You will need:
14" pillow form
1/2 yd. red/beige check fabric
1/2 yd. floral fabric
1/3 yd. green check fabric (or ribbon) for ties

1. CUT FABRIC: Cut two 15"x15" pieces of red/beige check fabric for pillow front and back. Cut two 15"x17 1/2" pieces of floral fabric.

2. MAKE PILLOW: Pin red check pillow front and back together. Sew around all sides with 1/2" seams, leaving an opening. Trim corners, turn right side out and insert pillow form. Hand stitch opening closed.

3. FABRIC TIES: Cut 6 strips of the green check fabric to 2 1/2" x 10". Fold both long edges into the center (wrong sides together) of each strip. Fold each strip in half lengthwise, turning in ends as you do so and stitch across ends and along the side. Hand sew pairs of fabric ties at equal and opposite points along the opening.

4. COVER: Fold down floral fabric 1 1/2" (along 15" side) and press. Sew close to the raw edge. Fold down another 1 1/2" and press edge. Sew close to edge again. Do the same for the other piece. Place right sides of floral pieces together, sew 1/4" around 3 sides (except hemmed edge). Trim corners and turn right side out.

5. Slip red checked pillow inside floral cover and tie fabric ties into bows.

Scotty

(page 23)

You will need:
14" pillow form
1/2 yd. red tartan plaid fabric
1/2 yd. black and white gingham fabric
6"x6" piece of black cotton fabric
6" yellow grosgrain ribbon - 3/8" wide
4 1/2 yds. red grosgrain ribbon - 1/2" wide
Fabric glue
Fusible web

1. FRONT: Cut two 15" squares of gingham for front and back. Pin right sides together. Sew 1/2" around all sides, leaving a 9" opening for pillow form. Press seams open, trim corners and turn right side out. Insert pillow form and hand stitch opening closed.

2. COVER: Cut two 14 1/2" squares of plaid fabric. Press under 1/4" all around. Press under another 1/2" and sew in 3/8" along outer edge.

DECORATE: Fuse webbing (p. 109) onto black fabric. Using pattern (p. 114) cut out Scotty dog and iron to plaid front. Appliqué on with black thread. Tie a yellow bow and tack to neck.

3. Cut red grosgrain into 16 - 10" pieces. Sew two ribbons to the underside of each plaid square. "Sandwich" gingham pillow between plaid squares.

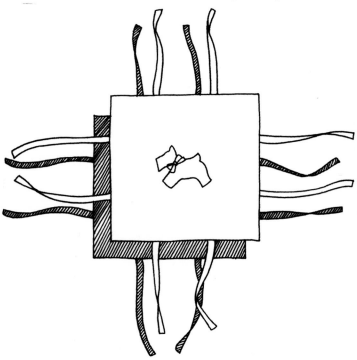

Tie together ribbons at sides into bows.

Organza Shadow Pillow

What a cozy place to curl up! Kitty dozes amidst billows of pillows. A white organza envelope covers a knife-edge pink gingham pillow, embellished with blue-checked covered buttons. Loops of organza keep the envelope snug. With the pink and white striped ruffled pillow and embroidered linens the grouping epitomizes understated good taste.

Organza Shadow Pillow
(page 25)

You will need:
14" pillow form
1/2 yd. white organza fabric
1/2 yd. pink/white check fabric
Scraps of blue/white gingham
3 - 1 1/8" flat button forms
Fray Check™ by Dritz®

1. CUT FABRIC: Cut two 15"x15" pieces of pink/white checked fabric for pillow front and back. Cut two 14 1/2"x16 3/4" pieces of organza.

2. FRONT: Pin checked fabric right sides together. Sew around all sides leaving an opening. Trim corners, turn right side out, and insert pillow form. Hand stitch opening closed.

3. COVER: Apply Fray Check™ along all sides of organza. Fold down 1 1/2" (along 14 1/2" side) and finger press. Sew close to the unfinished edge (A). Fold down another 1 1/2" and finger press edge (B). Sew close to edge again. Do the same for the other piece. Place right sides of organza pieces together, sew 1/4" around 3 sides (except hemmed edge).

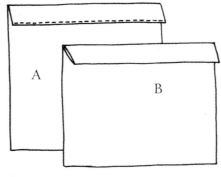

4. LOOPS: Cut three 1"x3" pieces of organza. Fold each in half lengthwise and finger press. Fold this length in half again and finger press. Sew close to open edge and turn right side out using a thin, blunt object.

5. BUTTONS: Cover buttons with blue/white checked fabric (following manufacturer's instructions) and sew to hemmed front edge of organza pillow front. Hand stitch loops to inside of pillow front at equal points along opening. Slip pink/white checked pillow inside organza cover and place loops around buttons.

Tip -
When sewing with very sheer fabrics such as organza, use an invisible thread (a clear nylon thread available at fabric and quilting stores.)

Tied up in ribbons

Lustrous satin, crisp taffeta, filmy organza, crinkly grosgrain, and wire-edged ribbons add personality to pillows you make for special settings. Wrap a pillow with a frothy floral bow; embellish a plain velvet pillow with a color-coordinated weave of bright ribbon strips; scrunch, bunch, wrap and tie ribbons to create one-of-a-kind pillow miracles. Ribbons are available in rainbow hues and a wide variety of sizes. With their finished edges they add that special final touch.

Floral Ribbon Rose
(page 29)

You will need:
14" pillow form
1/2 yd. floral fabric - 54" wide
3 yards transparent floral ribbon - 2 1/4" wide
2 yds. cable cord - 1/2" wide

1. CUT FABRIC: Cut one 15" square of floral fabric for front and two pieces 11"x15" for back.

2. DECORATE: Pin a 15" piece of ribbon across the center front, top to bottom. Cut two 27" pieces of ribbon. Pin and stitch one end of each on opposite sides of center front. Tie loose ends into a bow over center of other ribbon.

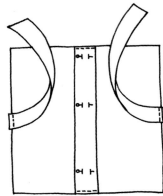

3. CASING FOR WELTING: Cut a bias fabric strip 120" long (see p. 104) 3" wide, piecing as necessary. Sew ends right sides together to form a circular strip. Fold in half lengthwise, right

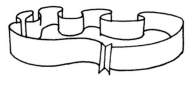

sides out. Pin and stitch (with a 5/8" seam allowance), leaving about a 6" opening at the center of this casing.

Insert cording using a large safety pin lead, scrunching the casing to fit. Pin

and stitch opening. Adjust gathers. Pin and stitch covered cord to front square, right sides together.

4. BACK: On wrong side of the two 11"x15" pieces, turn in a 1/2" hem on the long ends, press. Turn in another 1/2", press, pin and machine stitch close to edge. Remove pins. With right side facing up and hemmed edges on the inside, overlap the two back pieces by 5" so that they create one 15"x15" piece. Pin together along hemmed edges.

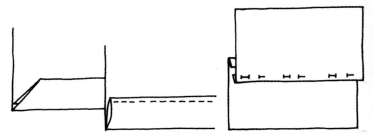

5. SEWING FRONT TO BACK: (Note: Use zipper foot to sew pillow) Pin the front to the back, right sides together. Sew a 1/2" seam allowance all around. Remove pins, trim corners, turn right side out and insert pillow form.

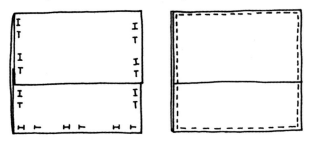

6. Make ribbon rose (see p. 110) and tack to center of pillow where the ribbons intersect.

Floral Ribbon Rose

For your English country house, or to wistfully add English country touches, this print adds old world charm! The knife-edge design, with a welt finish is wrapped with a transparent floral ribbon then embellished with a ribbon rose in the center. Lovely to look at and soft to touch.

Dainty Floral Bouquet
(page 31)

You will need:

18" pillow form

3/4 yd. pink brocade fabric

1/4 yd. off white batiste fabric (or other slightly
   transparent fabric)

1 yd. green ruffled trim

1 yd. pink picot ribbon trim

1 yd. rose gimp

4 pink tassels to match

3 yds. pink silk ribbon - 7mm

1 1/2 yds. pale yellow silk ribbon - 4mm

1 yd. burgundy silk ribbon - 4mm

1 yd. dusty green silk ribbon - 7 mm

1/2 yd. each light lavender and medium lavender
   silk ribbon - 4mm

Embroidery floss - dusty green

6" embroidery hoop

#24 chenille embroidery needle

Fusible web (optional)

1. RIBBON EMBROIDERY: Cut batiste fabric
7 1/2"x7 1/2". Complete ribbon embroidery
(see pattern and instructions on p. 111-112).

2. CUT FABRIC: Cut one piece brocade fabric
19"x19" and two pieces 13"x19".

3. FRONT: Sew or fuse embroidered piece to
pillow front. Sew or glue green gathered trim
around embroidered piece covering raw edges and
ruffling at corners. Turn under and join ends
neatly.

4. BACK: On wrong side of the two 13"x19"
pieces, turn in a 1/2" hem on the long ends, press.
Turn in another 1/2", press, pin and machine
stitch close to edge. Remove pins. With right side
facing up and hemmed edges on the inside, overlap
the two back pieces by 5" so that they create one
19"x19" piece. Pin together along hemmed edges.

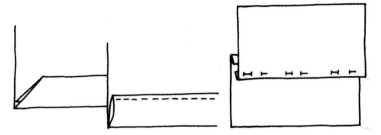

5. SEW FRONT TO BACK: Pin the front to the
back, right sides together. Sew a 1/2" seam
allowance all around. Trim corners, remove pins.
turn right side out and insert pillow form.

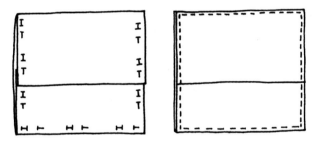

6. Glue pink picot trim over edge of green ruffled
trim. Miter corners either by folding or cutting.
Cut ends exactly where they meet and join with
glue. Glue pink rose gimp over the pink picot
trim. Tack tassels to each corner.

Tip -
If you would like to vary the embroidered
design of this pillow, consult your local craft,
fabric or needlework store. There are many
patterns available for silk ribbon embroidery.

Dainty Floral Bouquet

This stunning display of ribbon embroidery is enhanced by the large knife-edged pillow covered in rose brocade fabric finished off with matching silk tassels. The silk ribbon embroidered center was worked on white batiste, then sewn to the center of the pillow. Pale green ribbon trim, and floral gimp frame the beribboned handiwork. Elegant, and sophisticated, lovely ribbons have been used to create an extraordinary design.

Feathered Friends
(page 33)

You will need:
16" pillow form
Fabric panel - 8"x17" wide
1/2 yard striped fabric
Assorted silk ribbons - 2mm, 4mm, 7mm
Assorted embroidery floss
3 buttons for closures, about 1"
2 flower pot buttons
1 yard rickrack

1. CUT FABRIC: Cut striped fabric (A&B)
5 1/2"x18" and two pieces 7"x17".

2. ASSEMBLE:
Pin and stitch
striped fabric strips
A & B to front panel.

3. RIBBON
EMBROIDERY:
Embellish fabric
panel with silk
ribbon embroidery

stitches (see p. 111-112) - French knots, lazy daisy, etc. Use embroidery floss to feather stitch borders. Sew flower pot buttons to panel.

4. Fold case end strips (C&D) lengthwise, right sides out; pin and stitch to pillow front and pillow back ends, right sides together with 1/2" seam allowance.

5. Pin and stitch front to back on 3 unfinished sides, right sides together.

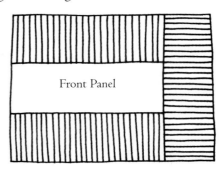

Trim corners, turn right side out, and add pillow form. Stitch closure buttons in place.

Tip -
While you may not be able to find the exact fabric panel we have used for Feathered Friends, there are many other printed fabric panels available. You could also use a border print fabric or fabric squares of an overall print pieced together for your own panel. Let the design of your fabric be your guide when adding silk ribbon embroidery stitches. Use the stitch instructions on page 112 and then go on to create your own unique design.

Feathered Friends

It is always Spring on this clever, fresh, green striped pillow! The printed border of birds has been added to the green striped fabric. For embellishment, part of the design has been ribbon embroidered. Embroidery also includes the trailing tendrils of vines. Novelty garden motif buttons add interest to the wide single-edge border.

Woven Satins

(page 35)

You will need:

14" pillow form

1/2 yd. velveteen

Assortment of ribbons in 13" lengths (18-20
  ribbons depending on widths)

2 yds. velvet ribbon - 1 1/4" wide

1/2 yd. fusible interfacing

1. CUT FABRIC: Cut velveteen in two 11"x15"
pieces. Cut interfacing 15"x15".

2. FRONT: Draw 12" square on interfacing. Pin
corners to a cork board or cardboard, adhesive side
up. Arrange vertical ribbons snugly side by side;
pin to top edge of square.

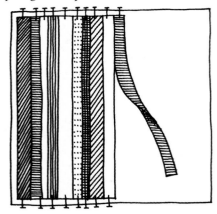

Working from the top, arrange and pin ribbons
across, alternating over and under verticals.

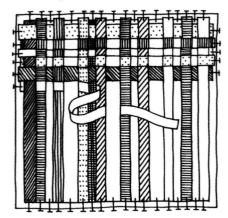

Weave to bottom. Using a press cloth over ribbons,
iron to fuse weaving to interfacing. Remove pins.
Press with steam iron from back.

3 BORDER: Cut velvet border ribbon into four
pieces 15" long. Pin this ribbon to each edge of
pillow front with right sides together - with 1
1/2" of ribbon extending on each side. Sew very
close to ribbon edge all the way to end of pillow
front, holding adjacent ribbon out of the way.

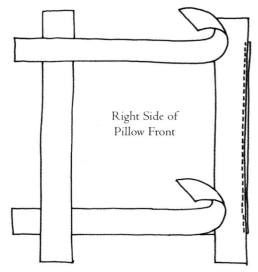

Right Side of
Pillow Front

4. MITER CORNERS:
Pull up ribbon ends and
align raw edges. Pin.
Machine stitch. Remove
pin. Cut off excess.
Open out. Press.

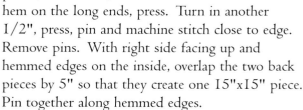

5. BACK: On wrong
side of the two 11"x15"
pieces, turn in a 1/2"
hem on the long ends, press. Turn in another
1/2", press, pin and machine stitch close to edge.
Remove pins. With right side facing up and
hemmed edges on the inside, overlap the two back
pieces by 5" so that they create one 15"x15" piece.
Pin together along hemmed edges.

6. SEW FRONT TO BACK: Pin front to back
and sew a 1/2" seam allowance all around. Trim
corners and turn right side out. Insert pillow
form.

Woven Satins

Beribboned to match your color scheme, any combination of ribbons can be used to create this woven pillow design. A rich, border of wine velveteen acts as a foil for the glowing hues of the ribbons. Use ribbon scraps to achieve a homespun effect, or carefully select contrasting colors and ribbon finishes for a highly artistic result.

Ribbon Framed Rose

Timeless yellow and white plaid serves as the backdrop for a large, cabbage rose print surrounded by softly gathered wire-edged ribbon. A ribbon rosette and button anchor the center design. Welt finish uses the same floral fabric. Distinctive and unusual, this decorative design compliments the simple yellow print, yet stands out from the white upholstered sofa fabric.

Ribbon Loops

Loops and loops and loops of wired-edged ombre ribbon in watercolor hues attached to a plain knife-edged pillow create this imaginative result! Artistic and provocative, this pillow will get admiring glances wherever you display it. Choose ribbons to enhance your color scheme, or make a Technicolor patchwork from scraps of ribbons recycled from gifts and hair bows!

Ribbon Loops

You will need:

14" pillow form

1/2 yd. fabric to match ribbons

3 yds. of various widths and colors of ribbon
  (we used wire edged)

1. CUT FABRIC: Cut one piece of fabric 15"x15" and two pieces 11"x15".

2. RIBBON: Cut ribbon into 8" pieces (to cover width of pillow front - approximately 110 pieces). Fold 10 -11 pieces in half. Pin along bottom of pillow front 1/2" in from edges and bottom. Sew along raw edges or ribbon. Remove pins.

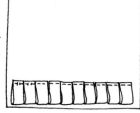

3. Add rows of folded ribbons in this manner, overlapping the stitches of the previous rows until you reach the top 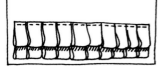 of the pillow front. The top row of ribbons should be even with the raw edge of the fabric.

4. BACK: On wrong side of the two 11"x15" pieces, turn in a 1/2" hem on the long ends, press. Turn in another 1/2", press, pin and machine stitch close to edge. Remove pins. With right side facing up and hemmed edges on the inside, overlap the two back pieces by 5" so that they create one 15"x15" piece. Pin together along hemmed edges and set aside.

5. SEW FRONT TO BACK: Lay pillow front on pillow back (right sides together). Pin or tape ribbons out of the way of stitching area. Sew front to back with 1/2" seams. Trim corners, turn right side out and insert pillow form.

(Tip: This is a great way to use up scraps of ribbon too pretty to throw away).

Ribbon Framed Rose
(page 36)

You will need:
14" pillow form
1/2 yd. yellow plaid fabric
1/2 yd. floral fabric
2 yds. cable cord - 1/2"
1 1/2 yds. wire edged ribbon - 1" wide
Decorative button
1/4 yd. fusible web
Fabric glue

1. CUT FABRIC: Cut plaid fabric into one 15"x15" piece and two 11"x15" pieces. Cut one piece of the floral fabric 7 1/2" x 7 1/2" (centering a rose).

2. MAKE WELTING: Cut enough 2" strips of the floral fabric on the bias to make 59" of welting (see p. 104). On the wrong side, fold in 1" at both short ends. Pin and press. Lay the strip wrong side up and place the cord in the middle lengthwise, leaving a 1" fabric overlap at one end. Fold fabric over cord, pin, with zipper foot stitch close to cord. Remove pins. Take both ends and make a circle. Tuck the cord inside the overlap and stitch across the joint. Fuse the floral square to the middle of the plaid fabric (see p. 109)

3. BACK: On wrong side of the two 11"x15" pieces, turn in a 1/2" hem on the long ends, press. Turn in another 1/2", press, pin and machine stitch close to edge. Remove pins. With right side facing up and hemmed edges on the inside, overlap the two back pieces by 5" so that they create one 15"x15" piece. Pin together along hemmed edges and set aside.

4. SEW FRONT TO BACK: Pin the welting around the back piece, raw edges together. Machine stitch in place. Pin the front and back, right sides together and machine stitch all around near the welting using 1/2" seam allowance. Trim corners and turn right side out.

5. RIBBON TRIM: Expose the wires at each end of the ribbon. Bend the two wires down at one end to keep in place. Pull the two wires at the other end to ruffle the ribbon. Do this gently to keep from breaking the wires. Ruffle up enough to fit around floral fabric square. Use fabric glue to glue in position, starting and ending at center bottom of floral square.

6. RIBBON ROSETTE: Cut ribbon 12" long. Expose one wire on one end. Bend down to hold in place. Expose the other end of this wire and pull to form a circle. Fold the end of the ribbon under and glue. Glue this at center bottom of floral square. Glue decorative button in the middle.

Just for the fun of it

Buttons, bows, stamps, a bit of this, a bit of that. Imagination soars in creating these remarkable examples of pillow magic. Pillows become art to grace a settee, bolster a color scheme, or add dramatic interest to a cozy corner. Poke through your sewing box for unusual buttons or trims; capture a moment in nature with a botanical imprint in paint; use softly glowing velvet, or shimmering satin to add a rich touch. Making these pillows is fun, and just the beginning of a creative flight of fancy.

Bows of Silk

Glowing pink taffeta covered in silk cord bows add sparkle to this knife-edge pillow. To finish the edges, the same silk cord is knotted, then hand stitched to the edge. For a teenager's room, imagine this pillow completed in her favorite colors, or school colors!

Felt Roses

Roses "bloom" on this brightly colored felt appliqued pillow. A bold blue and white checkerboard border adds homespun interest. Simple handstitching provides a folk-art feeling to this soft pillow.

Bows of Silk
(page 40)

You will need:
12" pillow form
1/2 yd. silk or satin fabric
Silk bands (assorted colors) from Arty's #SBC

1. CUT FABRIC: Cut fabric into 2 pieces 13"x13".

2. SEW FRONT TO BACK: Pin the two pieces right sides together. Sew together with 1/2" seam allowance, leaving opening to insert pillow form. Remove pins. Trim corners. Turn right side out.

3. DECORATE: Cut the silk bands in thirds and tie into about 20 bows. Make a small knot in each end. Sew on bows (see photo for placement). Insert pillow form and hand stitch opening closed.

4. Tie 2 lengths of 4 colors of bands together into one long piece about 84" long. Twist and knot about every 3 inches. Hand sew this all around the edge of the pillow.

Felt Roses
(page 41)

You will need:
12" pillow form
1/3 yd. white felt
1/4 yd. light blue felt
7" squares of pink, red, green, and denim blue felt
Embroidery floss - black and white
Fabric glue

1. CUT FABRIC: Cut two 12"x12" squares of white felt. Cut 32 - 1" light blue squares. Cut a 5 1/2"x5 1/2" light blue square and a 6 1/2"x6 1/2" denim blue square. Cut other felt pieces using patterns on p. 114.

2. DECORATE: Measure 1/2" all around outer edge and mark with pins. Glue blue checks to white background (see photo) staying within 1/2" of outer border. Blanket stitch larger blue square to center of pillow front with white floss. Stitch smaller blue square to this with white floss using a straight stitch. Glue roses to center. Stitch leaves around roses with black floss using straight stitch.

3. SEW FRONT TO BACK: Pin pillow front to back, right sides together. Sew around all sides with a 1/2" seam leaving one side open. Turn right side out, insert pillow and hand stitch closed.

Buttons Galore
(page 43)

You will need:
14" pillow form
1/2 yd. yellow and white polka dot fabric
2/3 yd. red and white gingham fabric
4 1/4 yds. red jumbo rickrack
12 medium red buttons
Fabric glue

1. CUT FABRIC: Cut a 15" square of yellow fabric for front and two pieces 11"x15" for back.

2. DECORATE: Glue rickrack to front fabric square. Begin by gluing from one corner to its diagonal corner. Glue second piece from the third corner to its diagonal corner, intersecting first rick-rack piece. Work off of these pieces, spacing each rickrack section about 2 3/4" apart. (Tip: Cut a 2 3/4"x17" paper pattern and use to space rick-rack strips.) Sew a red button in each square.

3. RUFFLE: Cut three 7"x38" strips of gingham. Sew each section together widthwise with a 1/2" seam. Press open seams. Fold gingham strip lengthwise, right sides together and sew with a 1/2" seam. Press open seams. Turn right side out and sew a running or gathering stitch 1/2" from sewn edge. Tighten gathers and pin to pillow front with gathered seam towards outer edges of pillow. Adjust gathers to fit. Sew on with a 1/2" seam.

4. BACK: On wrong side of the two 11"x15" pieces, turn in a 1/2" hem on the long ends, press. Turn in another 1/2", press, pin and machine stitch close to edge. Remove pins. With right side facing up and hemmed edges on the inside, overlap the two back pieces by 5" so that they create one 15"x15" piece. Pin together along hemmed edges.

5. SEW FRONT TO BACK: Pin pillow front to back, right sides together. Sew 1/2" seam around pillow over previously sewn stitches. Trim corners, turn right side out, and insert pillow form.

Buttons Galore

Ruffles, rickrack, buttons and color! Set against a sunny yellow fabric, with a red and white checked ruffle, this unexpected use of color and materials is perfect for a cozy, country setting. Use wide red rickrack, and shiny red buttons in primary colors with bright white to create impact, or choose a subdued palette for a more subtle look. Either way, this pillow is an interesting eye-full!

A Rose Is A Rose

No fancy stamps for this bouquet of roses! The cut end of a celery bunch was dipped in fabric paint to make the red, red rose. A single celery stalk dipped in contrasting green paint creates the leaves. Gold calligraphy ink strokes the quote by Gertrude Stein, "A rose, is a rose, is a rose." on the background of white. Finished off with a crinkly green plaid taffeta ribbon, the tribute is worthy of the famous poet.

Cherries Jubilee

Start with a cherry stamp in the center of this white pillow. Add a crisp frame of red ribbons, and a deep blue ruffle. Rubber stamps are easy to use, and offer a wide variety of design options. Choose strong, bold, images for impact as in this project. Vary the colors to match your color scheme. The clean design of the red and white, complimented by the soft ruffle, makes this pillow look comfortable--and it is!

45

A Rose is a Rose
(page 44)

You will need:
12" pillow form
1/2 yd. Muslin
2 1/2 yds. ribbon - green plaid - 2" wide
Paint (Delta Ceramcoat) Hunter Green, Tompte Red, Green Sea
Gold fabric marker
Fresh celery
Transfer Paper

1. CUT FABRIC: Cut one piece of muslin 13" x13" for front and two pieces 10"x13" for back.

2. DECORATE: Using pattern (p. 114) and transfer paper, transfer words repeatedly over entire pillow front. Trace over with gold marker.

3. Slice bottom off of a celery bunch. Take a few outer stalks off to make a smaller "rose". Dry, dip in red paint and stamp randomly on pillow front. (Practice first. You may need to rearrange some sections of the bunch to "open" spaces within rose image.)

4. Take one stalk and cut in half lengthwise. Round off the square cut end with a knife. Dip in two shades of green for each side of leaf and stamp around roses. Heat set paint (see p. 109).

5. RUFFLE: Sew a running or gathering stitch to top edge of ribbon. Gather up ribbon to match pillow top. Pin ruffle around pillow front, right sides together approximately 1/4" in from edge. Sew ruffle 1/2" in from edge.

6. BACK: On wrong side of the two 10"x13" pieces, turn in a 1/2" hem on the long ends, press. Turn in another 1/2", press, pin and machine stitch close to edge. Remove pins. With right side facing up and hemmed edges on the inside, overlap the two back pieces by 5" so that they create one 13"x13" piece. Pin together along hemmed edges.

7. SEW FRONT TO BACK: Pin pillow front to back, right sides together. Sew 1/2" seam around pillow over previously sewn stitches. Turn right side out, trim corners and insert pillow form.

Cherries Jubilee
(page 45)

You will need:
12" pillow form
1/2 yd. white cotton fabric
2/3 yd. bright blue chintz
3 1/2 yds. red satin ribbon - 3/8" wide
Rubber stamp - cherry (Rubber Stampede)
Paint (Delta Ceramcoat) red, green
Small paintbrush
Fabric glue

1. CUT FABRIC: Cut two 13" squares of white fabric for front and back.

2. DECORATE: Brush red and green paint onto cherry stamp with small brush. Test on paper first. Then reapply paint and stamp on center front of fabric. Heat set paint (see p. 109).

3. Cut eight 13" pieces of ribbon. Lightly glue outer ribbons 2 3/4" in from edges. Glue inner ribbons 1/2" from outer ribbons.

4. RUFFLE: Cut three 7"x33" pieces of blue chintz. Sew each section together widthwise, right sides together with a 1/2" seam. Press open seams. Fold chintz strip lengthwise, right sides together and sew with a 1/2" seam. Press open seams. Turn right side out and sew a running or gathering stitch 1/2" from sewn edge. Tighten gathers and pin to pillow front with gathered seam toward outer edges of pillow. (Ruffle edge should be flush with pillow edge.) Adjust gathers to fit. Sew ruffle on with a 1/2" seam.

5. SEW FRONT TO BACK: Pin pillow front to back, right sides together (ruffle to inside). Sew 1/2" seam around pillow, leaving an opening. Trim corners, turn right side out, insert pillow form and hand stitch closed.

Magical Leaves

This glowing jewel of velvet with its gathered edge finished in gold fringe, enhanced by magical leaves is easy to make. The "magic" is created by first placing a rubber stamp in the shape of a leaf under the velvet, followed by a mist of spray starch on the top surface over the stamp area. A hot iron pressed firmly on the fabric molds the velvet pile along the lines of the stamp. Select the rubber stamp motif to suit your theme for your own magic!

Magical Leaves
(page 47)

You will need:
12" pillow form
1/2 yd. green velvet
1 1/2 yds. gold plush fringe
Rubber stamp - oak leaf
Cotton pressing cloth

1. CUT FABRIC: Cut a 7"x13" piece of velvet for middle section. Cut two velvet strips 4"x18" for outer sections and a 13"x13" piece for back.

2. STAMP: (Test this technique on a small sample of velvet first. When you feel confident with the iron's heat and your technique, then begin on your larger piece of velvet). Heat iron to hottest setting (no steam). Place velvet face down on stamp (which is face up). Apply spray starch to velvet. Lay cotton pressing cloth on velvet and press with hot iron for 10 seconds. Repeat these steps, randomly stamping and ironing the velvet piece. (NOTE: Do not use foam stamps for this technique as they may melt with the heat of the iron. Hard rubber stamps work best.)

3. ASSEMBLE: Sew a gathering stitch along both long sides of each velvet strip.

Tighten gathers to measure 13" long. Pin strips to opposite sides of middle section, right sides together. Sew with a 1/2" seam.

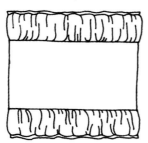

4. FRINGE: Pin fringe around pillow front about 1/4" in from edge (fringe side facing in).

Sew fringe down using a 1/2" seam.

5. SEW FRONT TO BACK: Pin pillow front to back with fringe to inside. Sew together with a 1/2" seam, leaving an opening. Trim corners, turn right side out, insert pillow form and hand stitch closed.

Tip -
Stamped Velvet

Shimmering, embossed velvet can be achieved at home for a fraction of the cost you would pay for the same thing at a fabric store.

Try other stamp images to create your own unique fabric designs. Stamps are available in a staggering variety. Try to find stamps that are not too detailed and have a more graphic look.

For the very best results - use rayon velvet. You will be amazed at the magical, glowing fabric you can create.

Patchwork

A piece of this, a scrap of that, bits of fabric, and forgotten quilt patches in a dusty attic box live again in keepsake pillows. Find vintage cloth at flea markets, estate sales, or buried at the back of grandmother's linen closet. Use these wonderful remnants of past times to embellish pillows in your home decor with memorable patterns, colors, and designs. Historical themes, contemporary compositions, or avant garde chic are simple to duplicate.

Floral Nine-Patch
(page 51)

You will need:
18" pillow form
1/2 yd. green/beige gingham
1/2 yd. green/ecru stripes
1/2 yd. rose and violet print
2 1/2 yd. mauve tassel trim

1. FRONT: Cut five 4 1/2"x4 1/2" squares of rose fabric and four squares of violet vintage fabric of same size. (Always sew patches with right sides together). Sew three fabric squares in a row, alternating prints (1/2" seams). Refer to photo for arrangements. Make three rows. Press open seams. Sew each row together with 1/2" seams. Press seams open. (Make sure two squares of the same fabric are not sewn side by side.)

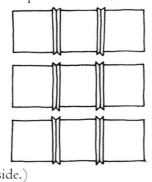

2. Cut two - 2"x11" strips of striped fabric and sew to sides of patchwork square, 1/2" seams. Press seams open. Cut two - 2"x13 1/2" strips of striped fabric and sew to top and bottom edge of square patchwork with 1/2" seams and press open.

3. Cut two - 3 3/4"x13 1/2" strips and sew to sides of pillow front. Press seams open. Cut two 3 3/4"x19" strips of green/beige gingham and sew to top and bottom of pillow front, press seams open.

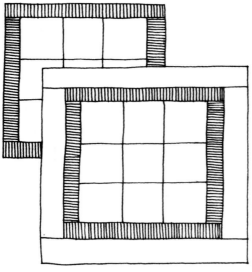

4. TRIM: Pin trim about 1/4" in all around pillow front, with bottom edge of trim facing outer edges. (It helps to tape it down with masking tape while sewing.) Sew down. Remove tape.

5. BACK: Cut two pieces of green/beige gingham 13 "x19". On wrong side of the two pieces, turn in a 1/2" hem on the long ends, press. Turn in another 1/2", press, pin and machine stitch close to edge. Remove pins. With right side facing up and hemmed edges on the inside, overlap the two back pieces by 5" so that they create one 19"x19" piece. Pin together along hemmed edges.

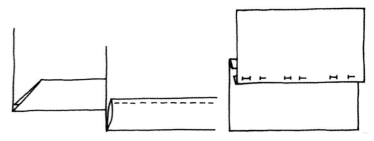

6. SEW FRONT TO BACK: Pin front to back pieces, right sides together. Sew around all sides with a 1/2" seam. Press seams open. Trim corners, turn right side out, and insert pillow form.

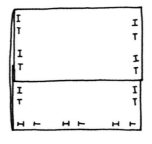 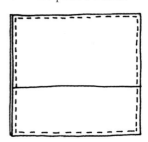

Floral Nine-Patch

Nine patches of a single fabric compose the artistic floral interpretation on this knife-edge pillow. A border of tiny checks and stripes draws your eye toward the center. Finished with a fringe of complimentary-colored tassels, the modern patchwork enhances the lines of this traditional sofa.

Patchwork Star
(p. 53)

You will need:
10" pillow form
1/3 yd. green gingham fabric
1/4 yd. purple fabric
1/4 yd. pink stripe fabric
1/4 yd. flowered fabric

1. CUT FABRIC: Cut fabric for front using patterns (page 115). Refer to photograph for directions of the stripes when cutting. Cut one piece of green gingham 11 1/2"x11 1/2" for back.

2. FRONT: Sew the pieces together (right sides together) in strips (as shown). See photo for directions of the stripes. Use 1/4" seams and press seam allowances before adding adjacent pieces.

Then sew the strips and pieces together in the order shown on the chart.

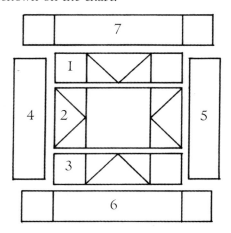

3. SEW FRONT TO BACK: Pin pillow front to back, right sides together. Sew all around with a 1/2" seam, leaving an opening. Trim corners, remove pins, turn right side out and insert pillow form. Hand stitch opening closed.

Tip -
For best results when making a pieced project, press every seam flat before another piece is sewn to it. The seams in patchwork are not pressed open but are pressed to one side. You'll have to decide which way seams should be pressed. This is a matter of common sense. For instance, press away from already bulky joints in previously sewn seams.

Patchwork Star

Historical patchwork "stars" in this combination of complimentary fabrics. A scrap from the upholstery material sets the color palette. Simple color patterns enhance the centerpiece, to create a memorable effect. Careful placement of the pieces insures authenticity of the vintage pattern.

Victorian Crazy Quilt

All things Victorian have a certain recognizable charm. This contemporary Victorian crazy quilt pillow, lush with silken bullion fringe, captures the Victorian era with its use of fabrics. Soft, glowing velvet, muted brocade, and watered silk taffeta linked with charming hand stitches looks and feels authentic. This lovely addition to your bed chamber grows more beautiful with age.

Silken Stripes

Lustrous bands of quilted taffeta, sewn in opposite directions form this simple knife-edge pillow. Poke through remnant boxes at fabric stores for materials to match your own coordinated color scheme, or look for unfinished quilting projects at tag sales. This pillow is as unique as your imagination, and easy to make!

Victorian Crazy Quilt
(page 54)

You will need:
18" pillow form
1/4 yd. each of vintage floral, burgundy velvet, moss green brocade, mauve brocade, pink satin
2/3 yd. burgundy brocade
1/4 yd. ecru lace - 3" wide
Large ecru doily
2 1/2 yd. mauve bullion fringe - 3" wide
Embroidery floss - mauve

I. FRONT: Cut fabric pieces using patterns (p. 119-120). Choose any crazy quilt piece and begin by sewing it, right sides together to its "neighboring" piece using a 1/4" seam. (Sew a doily or a piece of lace in a few places.) Press open seams. Repeat process until you have a complete pillow square. Recut if needed to a 19"x19" square. Add blanket, feather and straight stitches along fabric edges with mauve floss (see instructions for embroidery stitches - p. 110-111).

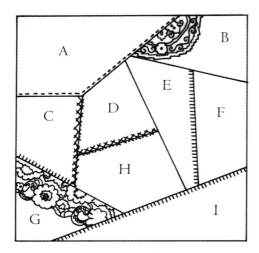

2. FRINGE: Pin fringe around pillow front so that fringe faces inward and bound edge of fringe is about 1/4" in from edge. Sew in 1/2" from edge.

3. BACK: Cut two 13"x19" pieces of the burgundy brocade. On wrong side of the two 13"x19" pieces, turn in a 1/2" hem on the long ends, press. Turn in another 1/2", press, pin and machine stitch close to edge. Remove pins. With right side facing up and hemmed edges on the inside, overlap the two back pieces by 5" so that they create one 19"x19" piece. Pin together along hemmed edges.

4. SEW FRONT TO BACK: Pin pillow front to back, right sides together. Sew a 1/2" seam all around pillow, leaving an opening. Trim corners, turn right side out. Hand stitch closed.

Silken Stripes
(page 55)

You will need:
12" pillow form
4 vintage quilt squares
1/2 yd. coordinating fabric for backing

I. FRONT: Lay first two squares together, pin and sew with 1/2" seams (right sides together). Press seams open. Make sure stripes are alternating, if using striped squares. Sew the other two squares together. Press open seams. Place the two pieces right sides together, and sew the blocks together. Press seams open.

2. BACK: Cut 2 pieces of backing fabric 10"x13". On wrong side of the two 10"x13" pieces, turn in a 1/2" hem on the long ends, press. Turn in another 1/2", press, pin and machine stitch close to edge. Remove pins. With right side facing up and hemmed edges on the inside, overlap the two back pieces by 5" so that they create one 13"x13" piece. Pin together along hemmed edges.

3. SEW FRONT TO BACK: Pin front to back, right sides together. Sew around all sides with a 1/2" seam. Press open seams. Trim corners, turn right side out and insert pillow form.

(Hint: Collect unfinished pieces of quilt squares. These can be found in antique stores, garage sales, swap meets, etc. They make wonderful pillows - or you may cut sections from damaged quilts.)

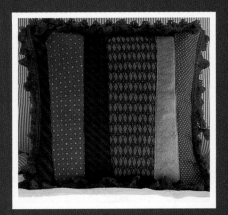

The Male Room

Comforting, strong, sturdy, and functional describe the projects in this chapter. Bold hues and textures, simple graphics, and symbols from nature, with practical touches are chosen for the pillows designed for men and boys. For a den, an antique reading chair, or just piled on a sofa for long hours of sports TV – the men in your life will cherish these pillows.

Dad's Ties

Rummage through any man's closet, and a treasure trove of fine old ties await a wonderful new life reborn as a quilted pillow. Choose favorite patterns, pieced together to keep memories alive and spark a smile, or carefully match colors for a coordinated effect. Either way, this simple pillow edged in burgundy tassels will be proudly displayed.

Reading Pillow

This sturdy, twill covered reading pillow boasts ribbon bands to keep book pages flat. Firmly attached strips of ribbon keep the book covers in place. Light weight, and portable, this pillow is the perfect gift for the bookworm in your life.

Dad's Ties
(page 58)

You will need:
14" pillow form
6 ties from thrift shops (or attic)
1/2 yd. black/brown small checked fabric
1 2/3 yds. burgundy tassel fringe
Thread to match each tie

1. CUT FABRIC: Cut a 15"x15" piece of checked fabric for front and two 11" x 15" pieces for back.

2. FRONT: Lay ties next to each other on top of 15" square, inverting every other one and slightly overlapping. Cut off tops and bottoms to match edges of fabric square. Pin ties down and sew close to edges with matching thread.

3. FRINGE: Pin tassel fringe around pillow front so that tassel band is about 1/4" in from edges, tassels facing inward. Sew on with a 1/2" seam allowance.

4. BACK: On wrong side of the two 11"x15" pieces, turn in a 1/2" hem on the long ends, press. Turn in another 1/2", press, pin and machine stitch close to edge. Remove pins. With right side facing up and hemmed edges on the inside, overlap the two back pieces by 5" so that they create one 15"x15" piece. Pin together along hemmed edges.

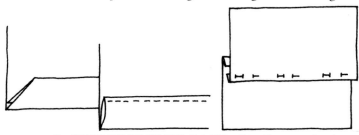

5. SEW FRONT TO BACK: Pin front to back, right sides together. Sew a 1/2" seam around pillow, over previous stitches. Trim corners, turn right side out and insert pillow form.

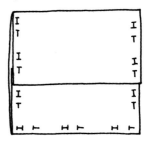
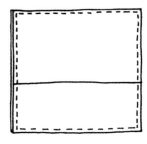

Reading Pillow
(page 59)

You will need:
18" pillow form
1 yd. fabric
2 - 20" pieces of ribbon - 1 3/8" wide
2 - 20" pieces ribbon (black satin) - 3/8" wide

1. CUT FABRIC: Cut two 20"x20" pieces of fabric.

2. FRONT: Mark a center point at bottom and top of pillow front. At 2 inches from the center top and bottom, pin wide ribbons in place. Measure 5 inches down on each side and pin narrow ribbon. Pin the other ends to the center mark.

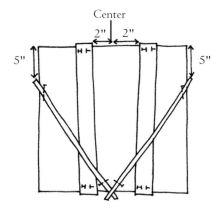

3. SEW FRONT TO BACK: Place the front and back fabric pieces right sides together and sew with 1" seam, leaving a 10" opening.

4. Trim corners, turn right side out and insert pillow form. Hand stitch opening closed.

5. Place book with pages open under the ribbons.

Natural Wonder

Nature's beauty is enhanced on this classic linen pillow. A deep green fern imprint is stamped in the center, then surrounded by barren twigs. Secure the twigs with heavy thread, leather, or twine to complete the natural effect. Propped among garden finds and collections this understated pillow is in elegant company.

Heartfelt

A warm pillow that says "I love you", is a comfortable find. Wide ribbed corduroy, fleece, and blanket-plaid flannel form a simple geometric. The red felt heart is appliquéd with a blanket stitch then anchored in the center by a leather thong tied off with tiny pine cones for a rustic patch of color.

Appliquéd Memories

Decidedly masculine images depicting favorite pastimes and hobbies embellish this soft,
comfortable pillow. Stitch up this cozy pillow for your Dad's favorite chair, a son's
dorm room, or that special quiet corner your grandson finds for reading. A patchwork
of old suiting material in nine complimentary colors make up the background. Leather
buttons, and boldly top-stitched bright wool symbols make this memorable gift unique.

Natural Wonder
(page 61)

You will need:
12" pillow form
1/2 yd. linen fabric
4 Twigs - 5" - 6" long
Brown embroidery floss
Rubber stamp - fern
Acrylic paint - green
Small brush

1. CUT FABRIC: Cut two 13"x13" squares.

2. DECORATE: Paint stamp green and stamp in center of one square.

3. SEW FRONT TO BACK: Pin pillow front to back. Sew around all sides with a 1/2" seam leaving an opening for turning. Trim corners, turn right side out, insert pillow form. Hand stitch opening closed.

4. Arrange four twigs around fern and stitch twigs down with brown embroidery floss.

Heartfelt
(page 62)

You will need:
12" pillow form
1/2 yd. brown polar fleece
1/4 yd. green polar fleece
1/4 yd. black and white large check flannel
7" square of dark red felt
10" leather strip
2 small pine cones
Embroidery floss - black
Hot glue gun and glue sticks

1. CUT FABRIC: Cut a 5"x13" piece of green polar fleece, a 6 1/2"x9" piece of black and white flannel and 7 1/2"x9" piece of brown polar fleece. Cut felt heart using pattern. Cut a 13" square of brown fleece for pillow back.

2. FRONT: With right sides together, sew black and white flannel piece to brown polar fleece with 1/2" seam. Sew green polar fleece to the side of this piece. Blanket stitch felt heart to center of fabrics with black floss.

3. SEW FRONT TO BACK: Pin pillow front to back, right sides together. Sew around all sides with 1/2" seams, leaving an opening for turning. Trim corners, turn right side out. Insert pillow form and hand stitch opening closed.

4. Cut a strip of leather. Tie a knot in center and ends. Sew center knot to heart center. Hot glue pine cones to end of knots.

Appliquéd Memories
(page 63)

You will need:
18" pillow form
9 squares of men's suiting fabric (from thrift shops or attic) - 7"x7" each
3/4 yd. backing fabric
Fabric scraps for appliqué
4 leather buttons, about 1"
4 suit buttons - about 1"
Doll or upholstery needle
Fusible web

1. CUT FABRIC: Cut backing fabric 19"x19". Cut assorted suiting fabrics into nine 7" pieces.

2. FRONT: Sew three squares together (right sides together) in a row with 1/2" seams alternating fabrics. Make three rows. Press open seams. Sew each row together with 1/2" seams. Press open seams.

3. DECORATE: Trace appliqué motifs (Patterns p. 113) to fusible webbing (see fusing instructions p. 109). Iron the appliqués to the fabric. Zig zag the edges using a sewing machine.

4. SEW FRONT TO BACK: With right sides together, pin pillow front to pillow back and sew up three sides with 1/2" seams. Trim corners, turn right side out and insert pillow form. Hand stitch opening closed.

5. To sew leather buttons to pillow front and suit buttons to back, mark center square on pillow back. Use a doll needle (or any extra long sturdy needle) to draw thread between corners of center square on front and back, pulling thread for slight pouf.

Sew Easy

Unexpected delight! When you need just the right color accent, these pillows solve the problem. Most are easy to make. Some use simple stitching techniques, or none at all! Each has its own unique purpose--adding a bright spot on a dark wooden bench, repeating a room theme, or adding an artistic touch. Make our projects, or adapt these designs to your own needs. Be careful, though, you may have so much fun, you won't be able to stop!

Easy No-Sew "Cheater" Pillow
(p.age 67)

You will need:
12" pillow form
1 yd. yellow floral fabric
1/2 yd. blue checked fabric
2 small rubber bands
Glue gun and glue sticks
3 large safety pins

1. CUT FABRIC: Cut yellow fabric 28"x28", and blue fabric 16"x30" and 5"x5".

2. ASSEMBLE: Center pillow form on wrong side of yellow fabric. Fold two edges of fabric over pillow, overlapping at center.   Use safety pins to secure (or use glue).

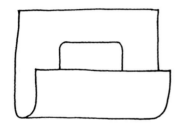

3. Fold the edges of the other two ends in.

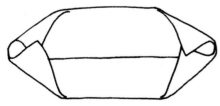

Then fold toward center and pin with safety pin (or glue).

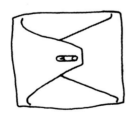

4. Fold up the long edges of the blue gingham fabric about 2" and press.

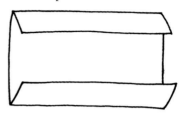

5. Lay the wrong side of the pillow on the wrong side of the blue gingham fabric. Pull the ends around to the front of the pillow.

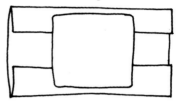

Wrap a rubber band around each end, tightly, gathering the fabric.

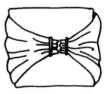

6. Fold the long edges of the 5"x5" blue fabric to meet in the back. Press. Wrap this piece around the two gathered ends of the other blue fabric and glue or pin in back, catching some of the gathered fabric.

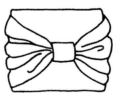

Easy No Sew "Cheater" Pillow

No sew pillow! Fun to make, and finished in minutes! A coordinating gingham fabric tied in a bow, covers the floral knife-edge pillow. Choose a floral fabric to match your color scheme, then add your own gingham touch! Only you will know you didn't sew!

Stars and Stripes

For this dramatic accent pillow, a hole was cut in the center of a pillow form. A fabric square was wrapped around the form, then stuffed into the center hole and embellished with striped fabric.

You will need:
16" pillow form   Fabric glue
1 yd. star fabric   Water glass
6"x20" contrasting fabric for center decoration

1. CUT FABRIC: Cut star fabric 36"x36". Cut striped fabric 6"x20".

2. PREPARE PILLOW FORM: Mark center of pillow form. Place a water glass on the center and trace around it to make a circle. Repeat on the other side. Sew around the circle and pull stitches tightly. Tie knot securely. Repeat on the other side.

Cut out the center of circle inside the stitches.

3. ASSEMBLE: Place the pillow form on top of fabric. Starting with one corner, tuck the fabric into the hole. Do the same with the other three corners. Glue fabric in the hole to secure.

4. DECORATE: Fold in long ends on the 6"x20" piece of striped fabric. Tie in loose knot. Stuff ends into hole and glue in position.

*B*each *Blanket Bingo*

Two large beach towels make up this patriotic salute to summer lazing. Choose any combination of beach towels to suit your pool side color scheme, add three pillow forms and comfort is an armful away from a nap! Sturdy, color-fast terry cloth stands up to sun, spills, and repeated washing. Dive in. This one is as easy as it looks!

Beach Blanket Bingo

You will need:
2 large beach towels approx. 20"x60" each
3 18" pillow forms
Velcro (optional)

1. With right sides out, sew across top and sides of the towels.

2. Measure the towel and divide by 3. Mark each division with pins. (Use masking tape to mark divisions and sew along edge of tape as a guide).

3. Sew along each division creating three equal "pockets".

4. Sew the bottom edge leaving an opening in each "pocket".

5. Open up the pillow forms and fill the three "pockets" with the loose filler. Use one form for each "pocket. This will give them all an equal fullness.

6. Sew the openings closed.

Harvest Envelope Pillow

Fun to make, and easy to look at, this envelope of bright fruit print and homespun basket weave fabric adds interest to the plain wooden furniture in this country kitchen. Make to match favorite kitchen linens, or coordinate with window coverings. Select a distinctive color, like the antique green paint on this chair, then find a fabric that matches. Envelope pillows are the simplest type to craft, so have fun with it!

From Towels to Pillows

Scour the grocery market, linens, or cookware shops for the fabrics used in these two clever bench pillows. Kitchen towels cover these easy-to-make pillows, picking up the hues from the rustic dining area furniture. Ribbon and a silk flower clasp the top of the sack pillow, while a vintage, embroidered doily embellishes the bolster.

From Towels to Pillows - Bolster
(page 71)

You will need:
14" pillow form (or 14" bolster pillow form)
2 dish towels 20"x30"
1 5"x45"matching or contrasting fabric
2 - 4" pieces of elastic
Optional: Antique embroidered doily

1. TO MAKE A BOLSTER PILLOW FORM:
Fold square pillow form in half and stitch by hand to form a cylinder.

2. ASSEMBLE PIL-
LOW: Cut towel to 15
1/2"x30". Fold towel in half lengthwise with right sides together and stitch with 1/2" seam. Sew long side of towel together with a 1/2" seam. Turn right side out. Tuck ends of towel inside about 2".

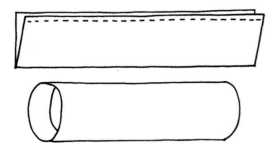

Slip pillow form into towel tube.

3. TO MAKE SCRUNCHIES: Cut the 5"x45" piece in half to 2 pieces 5"x22". Fold in half lengthwise right sides together. Sew 1/4" seam down side to form a 22 1/2" long tube.

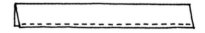

Press the seam so it is the center of one side. Turn right side out. Place elastic in one end of the tube. Sew across end about 1/4" in from end. Pull and stretch elastic inside the tube to the other end and sew across end of elastic and tube, also about 1/4" in.

Sew ends together forming a circle. Put this seam on the inside. Repeat these instructions for the second piece of fabric.

4. Slip scrunchies on ends of pillow.

5. If desired, add embellishment such as the antique embroidered doily.

Harvest Envelope Pillow
(page 71)

You will need:
16" pillow form
1 18" wide dish towel
1 18" x 18" napkin

1. Cut napkin in half on the diagonal.

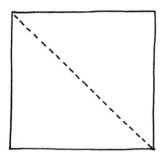

2. Mark the center of the towel at the top and center of the napkin on the long side and pin.

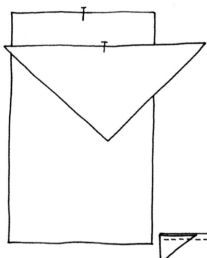

3. Match the two center marks. Pin towel and napkin together at top of towel, right sides together. Fold in corners of the napkin. Stitch across top with 1/2" seam.

4. Fold the towel in half widthwise with right sides together. Sew with 1" seams on each side. Turn right side out. Pull napkin flap out.

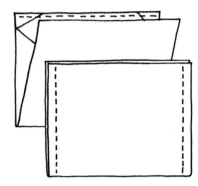

5. Insert pillow form into the "pocket" and hand stitch top of towel together.

6. Add button or charm to decorate, if desired.

From Towels to Pillows - Sack Pillow
(page 71)

You will need:
14" pillow form
20"x30" dish towel
45" matching ribbon
1 bunch silk flowers for embellishment

1. Fold towel right sides together to 15"x20". Sew up long sides of towel with 1/2" seams.

2. Turn right side out and slip in pillow form. Tie ribbon at top and add silk flowers to embellish.

(Tip: Look for pretty dish towels with printed or appliqued designs to make a variation of this pillow. Match the ribbon to the design of the dish-towel and add decorations such as wooden hearts, tassels, buttons, etc. to coordinate with the design on the towel.)

From Napkins to Pillows

Colorful, textured napkins coordinated to match your breakfast nook or table linens form this duo of simple-to-make pillows. Four fringed corners hand-stitched together over a firm pillow form look rustic and homespun. The companion pillow uses two similarly made napkins, yet boasts a deep flange. A row of stitching snugly encloses the pillow form. For added interest, an antique quilt square in complimentary colors has been appliqued on one side. Country chic in no time at all!

From Napkins to Pillows - Flange
(page 73)

You will need:
16" pillow form
2 napkins - 20"x20" with fringe
3 yds. household string
Needle - #18 chenille
Patchwork piece to embellish
24" burgundy gimp trim
Fabric glue

1. Thread needle with about 25 inches of string. (you may wish to substitute string with twine or narrow ribbon).

2. Place napkins wrong sides together. Hand stitch with string - on 3 sides 2" from edge. Stitch one side at a time leaving a long tail of string for tying bow. Leave one side open for pillow form.

3. Insert the pillow form. Re-thread needle and sew across bottom 2 inches up from edge. Tie bows in all four corners.

4. Sew or fuse embellishment to center of pillow. (We used a vintage patchwork square). Glue or hand stitch gimp trim around edge.

Tip -
This would be a good project for teaching a young child to sew.

From Napkin to pillows - Fringed
(page 73)

You will need:
21" x 21" napkin with fringe
14" pillow form
Needle

1. Place pillow form in the middle of the napkin on a diagonal.

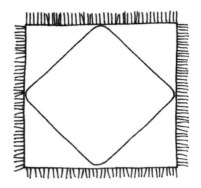

2. Fold one corner to the center of pillow form and pin. Bring up the other 3 corners one at a time and pin.

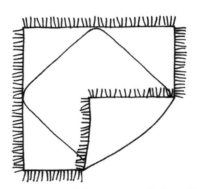

3. Starting at one outside corner of the pillow, hand stitch both sides of napkin together right below the fringe - up to the center of the pillow. Repeat with the other 3 corners.

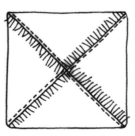

Bits and Pieces of Old

A bit of this, a piece of that. Forgotten scraps of fabric and trims spill out of of your sewing basket, just begging for life! Sort them and plan. Find complimentary remnants at fabric shops. Poke through vintage linens at tag sales and dusty trunks in antique stores. Neglected needlework projects, half-finished quilts, castoff table and bed linens are treasures just waiting to be found. These creative projects use bits and pieces, and imagination!

Flower Girl

A bit of blue and red trim frames the vintage needlepoint lady examining the red rose on this pillow. Both the solid field of blue, and gingham match her fluttering dress perfectly, and the heavy white cotton bullion fringe cleanly finishes this country picture.

Needlepoint Gardener

Like a French parterre garden, this pillow contrasts measured rows of fine green checks against a glorious floral explosion. Various burgundy trims keep order along with the little needlepoint gardener in the center of things! Antique needlepoint was used in this example, but a bit of printed fabric or new needlework would be fine in this pillow garden.

Flower girl
(page 76)

You will need:
18" pillow form
1/2 yd. blue gingham fabric
1/4 yd. solid blue fabric
Piece of vintage needlepoint (can be found in antique stores, garage sales, second hand stores, grandma's attics)
1/2 yd. braided cord
2 yds. white bullion fringe
Fusible web
Fusible seam tape

1. CUT FABRIC: Cut needlepoint piece in oval shape (pattern p. 121) Put a little glue around edge to keep from unraveling. Cut one piece solid blue fabric 12"x12 1/2". Cut one piece blue gingham fabric 19"x19" and two pieces 13"x19".

2. FRONT: Turn under edges 1/2" of the blue square and use iron-on seam tape to hem. Fuse to blue gingham fabric. Fuse needlepoint piece to blue fabric.

3. BACK: On wrong side of the two 13"x19" pieces, turn in a 1/2" hem on the long ends, press. Turn in another 1/2", press, pin and machine stitch close to edge. Remove pins. With right side facing up and hemmed edges on the inside, overlap the two back pieces by 5" so that they create one 19"x19" piece. Pin together along hemmed edges.

4. FRINGE: Pin fringe around pillow front about 1/4" in from edge (fringe side facing in). It helps to tape it down with masking tape while sewing.

5. SEW FRONT TO BACK: Pin pillow front to back with fringe to inside. Sew together with 1/2" seam. Trim corners, remove tape and pins.

6. Turn right side out and insert pillow form.

Needlepoint Gardener
(page 77)

You will need:
18" pillow form
3/4 yd. floral fabric
1/3 yd. green check fabric
2 1/4 yds. burgundy ball fringe
1 1/3 yds. burgundy gimp trim
1/2 yd. burgundy flower trim
Vintage needlepoint piece (can be found at garage sales, flea markets, antique stores, etc.)

1. CUT FABRIC: Cut one piece floral fabric 19"x19" and two pieces 13"x19". Cut one piece green check fabric 11"x11".

2. FRONT: Center green check fabric on floral fabric, pin, stitch. Trim any rough edges of needlepoint piece and center on green checked piece. Pin. Stitch in position. This could also be fused on, if desired. Glue or stitch burgundy gimp around green checked fabric, covering raw edges. Glue or stitch the burgundy flower trim around the needlepoint piece covering raw edges.

3. BACK: On wrong side of the two 13"x19" pieces, turn in a 1/2" hem on the long ends, press. Turn in another 1/2", press, pin and machine stitch close to edge. Remove pins. With right side facing up and hemmed edges on the inside, overlap the two back pieces by 5" so that they create one 19"x19" piece. Pin together along hemmed edges.

4. FRINGE: Pin ball fringe to pillow front, 1/2" in all around and sew down. (Bottom edge of trim faces outer edge of pillow front.)

5. SEW FRONT TO BACK: Pin the front to the back, right sides together. Sew a 1/2" seam allowance all around. Trim corners, remove pins, turn right side out and insert pillow form.

Buttons and Lace

A vintage doily is embellished with old buttons, then placed "just so" over black fabric. A crisp checked black and beige linen centers this pillow and repeats on the welt edge. The contrasting band of cluny lace over tea-dyed muslin combines both old and new to showcase a reminder of yesteryear. Can't find vintage crochet work? Tea dye a new piece, no one will ever know!

Buttons and Lace
(page 79)

You will need:
14" pillow form
1/2 yd. muslin
1/4 yd. black/beige gingham
5 3/4"x5 3/4" black ultra suede
5 1/2" crochet doily
60" cable cord - 3/8" thick
12 medium brown buttons
1 1/4 yd. cluny lace
Fabric glue

1. CUT FABRIC: Cut two 15"x15" squares of muslin. Cut one 9" square of gingham and one 5 3/4" square of black ultra suede. Tea stain muslin and doily (see p. 109).

2. FRONT: Press 1/4" under all around gingham square. Center gingham onto pillow front, pin and machine stitch down. Machine stitch ultra suede square in center of gingham (see photo for placement). Sew doily onto black square with matching thread. Sew a button onto each scallop and center of doily. Glue lace around gingham square, mitering each corner.

3. WELTING: Cut three 3"x20" strips of gingham on the bias. Sew together into 60" strip. Press seams open. Fold gingham strip wrong sides together, "sandwiching" cord. Pin and sew close to cord and sew with a zipper foot.

4. Pin and sew welting around pillow front so that the edge of cord is 1/2" from pillow edge. Where welting ends meet, tuck raw edge inside overlap. Stitch across joint.

5. SEW FRONT TO BACK: Pin pillow front to back, right sides together. Sew together, sewing over 1/2" seam along welting. Trim corners. Leave an opening and turn right side out. Insert pillow form and hand stitch closed.

Vintage Fabrications
(page 81)

You will need:
18" pillow form
8 squares vintage fabric (or reproduction fabric), 7"x7" each
1 vintage embroidered square - 7"x7"
3/4 yd. backing fabric
1 yd. rickrack, large
1 yd. rickrack, medium
2 yds. rickrack, mini

1. FRONT: Arrange fabric squares around center piece.

2. Pin and sew squares together (right sides together) with 1/2" seams. Press seams open in panels of 3 squares each.

3. Pin and stitch top panel to middle panel, then to bottom panel, matching seams. Press seams open.

4. Machine stitch large rickrack over both vertical seams. Stitch medium rickrack over both horizontal seams. Hand stitch mini rickrack on top of these strips of larger rickrack.

5. BACK: On wrong side of the two 13"x19" pieces, turn in a 1/2" hem on the long ends, press. Turn in another 1/2", press, pin and machine stitch close to edge. Remove pins. With right side facing up and hemmed edges on the inside, overlap the two back pieces by 5" so that they create one 19"x19" piece. Pin together along hemmed edges and set aside.

6. Pin the front to the back, right sides together. Sew a 1/2" seam allowance all around. Remove pins. Trim corners, turn right side out and insert pillow form.

Vintage Fabrications

Capture a timeless moment in this comfy pillow. Center a hand-embroidered scrap of linen amidst squares of cheerful, nostalgic 1940s fabric. Bands of perky rickrack in complimentary colors finish this "old softie".

Unfinished Symphony
(p.age 83)

You will need:

12" pillow form

12"x12" needlepoint canvas (we used a piece with an unstitched background, easy to find at garage sales)

1 3/4 yds. chintz fabric, 54" wide (colors to coordinate with needlepoint)

1 1/2 yds. cable cord - 1/2" wide

NOTE: If the canvas background is unstitched, pin and stitch edge of 13" square of chintz, right side up, behind the needlework.

1. RUFFLE: Cut or tear two 8" wide strips of chintz across the width (54") of the fabric. Pin and stitch the ends right sides together, to form a circular strip. Fold the strip in half lengthwise, right sides out. Mark the midpoints between 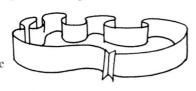 the seams to divide into four equal sections. Baste each section in 2 rows (1/4" apart); pull up the thread, gathering to a 12" size. Pin and stitch the ruffle to the canvas, right sides together.

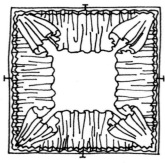

2. WELTING: Cut a 56"x1 1/2" wide strip of chintz on the bias piecing as necessary (see p. 104). Fold strip in half lengthwise, right sides together. Stitch 1/4" from the raw edge, forming a casing 1/2" wide. Turn casing right side out. Thread the cord through the casing using a safety pin as a lead.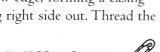

Pin cord around ruffle where it meets the canvas on pillow top. Begin at the bottom middle, pinning the center of the cord there and stitch it by hand in either direction until it meets at top center. You will have about 7" excess on each end. Hand stitch the cord in place. Tie a knot with the ends, turning under to form loops. Tack in place.

3. Pin ruffles toward center front to keep them free as you finish pillow backing. Hand tuck the cord in place. Tie a knot with the ends, turning under to form loops. Tack in place.

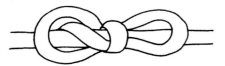

4. BACK: On wrong side of the two 10"x13" pieces, turn in a 1/2" hem on the long ends, press. Turn in another 1/2", press, pin and machine stitch close to edge. Remove pins. With right side facing up and hemmed edges on the inside, overlap the two back pieces by 5" so that they create one 13"x13" piece. Pin together along hemmed edges.

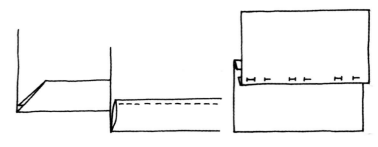

5. SEW FRONT TO BACK: Pin the front to the back, right sides together. Sew a 1/2" seam allowance all around. Trim corners, turn right side out, remove pins and insert pillow form.

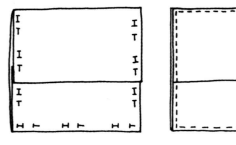

Unfinished Symphony

Blue butterflies pause on a sprig of dill in this unfinished needlepoint sewn atop the pillow fabric. The wide ruffled edge frames the dimensional artistry. For a garden room, a sunny spot to relax and read, or to just showcase the stitching, this focal point gets attention.

Memory Patches

Memory quilt squares are the focal point of this bright red and white pillow grouping. Look for stitched squares among antique linens at flea markets, or embroider your own to create new family heirlooms. Keep the colors coordinated, use simple stripes and squares to draw attention to the embroidery, add ruffles to soften the theme for a country bed.

God Bless America

This patriotic setting started with the purchased pillow on the left. To add balance, the second pillow made from red checked fabric, extends the theme with a hand-embroidered vintage sampler in the middle.

God Bless America

You will need:
16" pillow form
1 vintage embroidered piece (approx. 9" x 12")
1/2 yd. plaid fabric
Fusible web

1. CUT FABRIC: Cut the plaid fabric into one 17"x17" piece, and two 12"x17" pieces.

2. FRONT: Stitch or iron (using fusible web) embroidered piece to the 17"x17" piece.

3. BACK: On wrong side of the two 12"x17" pieces, turn in a 1/2" hem on the long ends, press. Turn in another 1/2", press, pin and machine stitch close to edge. Remove pins. With right side facing up and hemmed edges on the inside, overlap the two back pieces by 5" so that they create one 17"x17" piece. Pin together along hemmed edges.

4. SEW FRONT TO BACK: Pin the front to the back, right sides together. Sew a 1/2" seam allowance all around. Trim corners, turn right side out, remove pins and insert pillow form.

Lacy Velvet Neck Roll

Tuck this pretty confection made from bits and pieces of old lace and ribbons against a chair arm, or a pile of bed pillows. Velvet, wire-edged ribbon, a button and tassel in muted colors compliment upholstery fabric, or bed linens.

Folk Art Sampler

Display a favorite cross stitch sampler, yours or a tag sale prize, in the center of coordinating plaid. Surround the folk art needlework with burgundy gimp trim, then finish the pillow off with large mother-of-pearl buttons sewn along each edge.

Lacy Velvet Neck roll
(page 86)

You will need:
14" Bolster pillow form
20" square velvet
Vintage lace - petticoat bottom or pillow edge
2 - 1 yard pieces wire edged ribbon - 1 1/4" wide
2 - 3" squares of coordinating fabric
2 tassels to match fabric

1. Expose the wire on one end of the wire-edged ribbon and fold down to hold in place. Expose the same wire on the other end and pull carefully to gather up to 20". Do the same to the other ribbon. Pin gathered edge 3" from each side of velvet piece. Stitch.

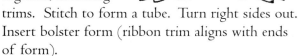

2. Working from the center of the velvet square, pin and stitch lace working out to ribbon edge and leaving about 1" of velvet exposed in the center.

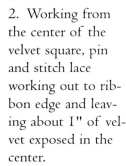

3. Fold velvet in half, right sides together, matching trims. Stitch to form a tube. Turn right sides out. Insert bolster form (ribbon trim aligns with ends of form).

4. Sew a gathering stitch at each end of velvet tube. Pull tightly to cover bolster ends. Knot and tack in place.

5. With the 3" squares of fabric, make yo-yos by

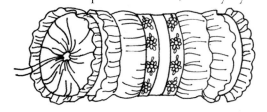

turning in the edge about 1/8" and sewing a gathering stitch. Pull up and knot. Glue or tack these to the ends of the bolster, covering the gathered end. Tie tassels around each yo-yo.

Folk Art Sampler
(page 87)

You will need:
16" pillow form
1 yd. plaid woven fabric (not printed)
6 buttons - 1"
Stitched cross stitch piece of your choice
1 yd. gimp trim
Fabric glue

1. CUT FABRIC: Cut 2 pieces of fabric 17"x32".

2. FUSE: Fuse cross stitch piece to center of one piece of fabric.

3. On cross stitch side, fold each end 3" toward cross stitch and press. Then another 3", press. Repeat this on second piece of fabric.

4. Place fabric together with folded "cuffs" on inside. Align cuffs and pin.

5. Sew up each long end with 1/2" seams. Turn right side out.

6. Insert pillow form. Sew three buttons on each cuff which will enclose pillow form inside. Sew or glue Velcro under buttons on one end of the pillow form to allow the form to be removed for cleaning.

7. Glue gimp trim around edge of cross stitch piece.

Gifts of Love

Hand crafted, home made, made by hand--no matter what you call it, a gift of love, comprised of thought and time is priceless. No greater tribute exists than to give a loved one, family friend, or relative something especially made for them. And, what better gift than one that provides comfort, color, and memories. To commemorate a family event, a wedding, new baby, or birthday, or as an insightful holiday gift, these pillow projects are distinctive and personal.

Family Album

Cherished family photos are grouped around an elegant monogram in this pillow designed for the caned-back chaise. Photographs in sepia transferred to muslin with pinked edges are appliqued to black ultra suede then fused to the khaki pillow. A loop of black silk braid glued in the center forms the monogram. Repeat the braid on the edges, add black tassels, and this family memento is complete.

Portrait Pillows

Combine vintage fabric, ribbons, tassels, and family photo transfers in two shapes for an appealing grouping. Photos can be prepared in black and white, antique sepia, or full color. These very special mementos contrast old black and white photos, with colorful fabric of the same era.

Vintage Memory Neckroll

You will need:

Bolster pillow form

1/3 yd. vintage floral fabric

1 yd. green/ivory striped fabric

1 1/4" black and white ribbon - 7/8"

Iron-on transfer of photo (ironed onto muslin)

7/8" fusible tape

2 chair tie with tassels - green

1. CUT FABRIC: Cut vintage fabric into one 9"x20" piece. Cut two 13 3/4"x20" pieces of striped fabric. (Make sure when cutting striped fabric that stripes run parallel with shortest length.)

2. Pin striped panels to center floral fabric, right sides together. Sew with a 1/2" seam. Press open seams. Press outer sides of striped fabric panels under 1/4". Fold back another 4", press and sew along 1/4" edge. (Continued on page 92)

3. Fuse gingham ribbons down with fusible tape on top of seam dividing vintage and striped fabric. Applique iron-on transfer to center panel.

4. Fold entire fabric piece lengthwise, right sides together and sew a 1/2" seam. Press open seams. Trim corners, turn right side out. Insert pillow form into center of tube. Tie ends with chair ties.

Family Album
(p.age 90)

You will need:
18" pillow form
2/3 yd. khaki fabric
1/4 yd. black ultra suede
2 1/8 yds. black cord - 3/8" wide
1/3 - 1/2 yds. black cord - 3/16" wide (depends on monogram size)
4 Large black tassels
Iron-on transfers of photos (ironed onto muslin)
Pinking shears
Fabric glue

1. CUT FABRIC: Cut a 19" square of khaki fabric and two pieces 13"x19".

2. FRONT: Iron transfers to muslin (see p. 109). Cut muslin photo transfers into ovals (patterns p. 121) and rectangles using a pinking shears. Cut out black ultra suede shapes slightly larger than muslin photos. (Spread glue over back of muslin photos with a craft stick, making sure each point is glued. Glue these to ultra suede pieces.) Arrange photos on top of pillow front and lightly tape down. Machine appliqué each one with black thread.

3. INITIAL: Use the family initial (see alphabet p. 116-117). Enlarge letter on copy machine and use as a pattern. Lay cord on pattern to determine size to cut cord. Glue on each end to keep it from unraveling. Center pattern on pillow and poke dots through with a sharp pencil, transferring letter design to pillow front. Squeeze a line of glue over letter pencil dots and lay 3/16" cord in glue.

4. SEW FRONT TO BACK: Pin pillow front to back, rights sides together. Sew all around with a 1/2" seam leaving an opening. Trim corners, remove pins, turn right side out and insert pillow form. Hand stitch opening closed.

5. Glue 3/8" cord around pillow over seam. Glue edges of cord to prevent unraveling. Butt ends together and glue.

6. Glue or sew tassels to corners.

Portrait Pillow
(page 91)

You will need:
12" pillow form
Photo ironed onto muslin fabric (or iron-on transfer of photo on muslin)
1/2 yd. vintage floral fabric
1/4 yd. green stripe fabric
2/3 yd. black and white plaid ribbon - 7/8" wide
Black tassel
Fusible tape - 7/8" wide

1. CUT FABRIC: Cut two 13"x13" squares of floral fabric for pillow front and back. Cut 2 pieces of striped fabric using pattern (p.122).

2. MAKE FLAP: Put the two pieces of striped fabric together, right sides together and sew with 1/2" seam, leaving the top open. Turn right side out. Iron strips of ribbon along edges of flap with fusible tape. Miter corner.

3. SEW: Center and pin flap to right side of pillow back. Pin pillow front on top of this, right sides together. Sew around all sides with 1/2" seams leaving an opening at bottom. Trim corners, turn right side out and press.

4. Appliqué iron-on transfer to center flap. Sew a tassel to underside of flap.

5. Insert pillow form and hand stitch closed.

Lavender and Lace

Stitch up a romantic treasure from watery blue moire and a silk ribbon embroidered handkerchief, dripping in lace. A pocket of moire makes a perfect place to tuck a lavender sachet made from the same lacy hanky. Tie the sachet with a ribbon to match the embroidery. For mother's day, this sweet gift will be a treasured keepsake.

Lavender and Lace
(page 93)

You will need:
12" pillow form
1/2" yd. blue moiré fabric
White handkerchief
1 yd. silk ribbon - lavender, 4mm wide
Embroidery floss - lavender, green
Needle - #24 chenille
Lavender, loose buds (or potpourri mixture)

1. CUT FABRIC: Cut one piece moiré fabric 13"x13" for front and two pieces 10"x13" for back. Cut one piece 5 1/2"x5 1/2" for pocket.

2. POCKET: Fold in all edges 1/4", press and pin. Cut handkerchief as shown in illustration. Embroider using pattern (p. 118). Glue on small lavender silk bow. Place handkerchief corner on pocket. Pin. Wrap top and side edges to back of pocket. Pin. Center and sew pocket to pillow front using blue thread on the blue fabric and white for the handkerchief.

3. BACK: On wrong side of the two 10"x13" pieces, turn in a 1/2" hem on the long ends, press. Turn in another 1/2", press, pin and machine stitch close to edge. Remove pins. With right side facing up and hemmed edges on the inside, overlap the two back pieces by 5" so that they create one 13"x13" piece. Pin together along hemmed edges.

4. SEW FRONT TO BACK: Pin the front to the back, right sides together. Sew a 1/2" seam allowance all around. Trim corners, remove pins, turn right side out and insert pillow form.

5. LAVENDER POUCH: From remaining handkerchief fabric, cut a piece 3 3/4"x10", taking advantage of the already hemmed handkerchief. Fold in half wrong sides together and stitch with 1/4" seams, leaving top open. Thread the lavender silk ribbon in the needle and run it through the top of the pouch about 1 1/4" from top. Fill pouch with lavender and pull up the gathers and tie in a bow. Place in pocket.

(Tip: The lavender can be refreshed by adding lavender oil.)

Wedding Memory Pillow
(page 95)

You will need:
16" pillow form
1/2 yd. white moiré fabric
Assortment of pearls, doilies, buttons, laces,
  ribbon roses, and trims
2 gold rings
Fusible web
Fabric glue
Iron-on transfer of wedding announcement

1. CUT FABRIC: Cut one 17"x17" square of white moiré fabric for front and two pieces 12"x17" for back.

2. FRONT: Photocopy wedding announcement onto iron-on transfer paper and iron onto fabric front (see p. 109). Glue flat braid around announcement. Embellish the rest of the pillow as desired (or see photo for examples). Glue doilies, sew on groupings of buttons, iron on sections of sheet lace using fusible webbing, etc. Tie a bow of shear ribbon and glue to top of announcement. Twist, fold and sew ribbon down in a few places. Sew or glue a large ribbon rose to center of bow and sew a few small roses onto ribbon. Add any personal touches that give meaning to the bride and groom.

3. FRINGE: Pin white fringe around embellished pillow front (bottom edge of fringe along outer edges of pillow) about 1/4" in from edges. Sew with a 1/2" seam.

4. BACK: On wrong side of the two 12"x17" pieces, turn in a 1/2" hem on the long ends, press. Turn in another 1/2", press, pin and machine stitch close to edge. Remove pins. With right side facing up and hemmed edges on the inside, overlap the two back pieces by 5" so that they create one 17"x17" piece. Pin together along hemmed edges.

5. SEW FRONT TO BACK: Pin the front to the back, right sides together. Sew a 1/2" seam allowance all around. Remove pins, trim corners, turn right side out and insert pillow form.

Wedding Memories

Commemorate a wedding or anniversary with these mementos of the event. The invitation has been transferred to fabric then appliqued with a border of lace. Satin posies representing the bride's bouquet, golden rings, even pearls and buttons reminiscent of the gowns, add to this touching pillow. For the new bride and groom, or the twosome renewing their vows, this thoughtful gift will be treasured.

Alternative Bulletin Board

Crisscrossing ribbons in contrasting colors make up this soft, and easy to hold bulletin board! Slip favorite photos of pals, a treasured invitation to the prom and your escort's boutonnière. Display this in your favorite teen's room to become a lasting showplace of mementos and souvenirs.

*S*leepy-Time Pillows

Comfy and cuddly for nap time, and beyond, these two pillow gifts for baby will become
cherished possessions. A soft, cushy chenille square cut from an antique remnant, is
rimmed in baby blue tassels. Accompanied by a matching pillow covered in a whimsical
jersey knit sleeper, there's no mistaking these gifts from the heart are for the nursery.

Alternative Bulletin Board
(page 96)

You will need:
14" pillow form
1/2 yd. blue cotton fabric
1 2/3 yds. prairie points trim - pink
2 yds. grosgrain ribbon - light blue, pink and white
- 3/8" wide

1. CUT FABRIC: Cut two 15" squares of fabric.

2. FRONT: Lay pink ribbon from one corner to its opposite corner. Lay the blue ribbon from remaining corner to its opposite corner. Lay other ribbons down, parallel to these about 4" apart. (Tip: Cut a strip of paper about 4" x 17". Lay strip of paper along ribbon edges and use as a guide to place each length of ribbon.) Pin down ends of ribbons and where ribbons intersect.

3. Cut 8" lengths of ribbon. Tie bows and tack where ribbons intersect.

4. TRIM: Pin trim around pillow front with points facing inward and flat edge about 1/4" from pillow edge.

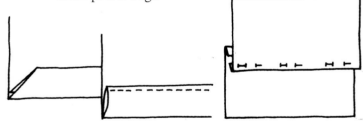

5. SEW FRONT TO BACK: Pin pillow front to back, right sides together. Sew around all sides with a 1/2" seam, leaving an opening. Trim corners, turn right side out, insert pillow form and hand stitch closed.

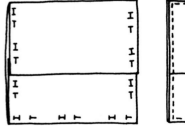

6. Place your favorite photos and mementos under ribbons.

Sleepy Time - Sleeper
(page 97)

You will need:
12" pillow form
Baby sleeper
Matching fabric for neck opening

1. Center a 13" square paper pattern over sleeper and pin in place. Cut out a front and back from the sleeper.

2. Pin right sides together. Sew front to back with a 1/2" seam, leaving an opening at bottom. Turn right side out, insert pillow form and hand stitch opening closed.

3. Cut a small piece of matching fabric to slip into the neck opening. Tack in place.

Sleepy Time - Chenille
(page 97)
You will need:

12" pillow form
Chenille blanket or bedspread (or new chenille panel)
1 1/3 yd. ball fringe, light blue

1. CUT FABRIC: Find a nice area on a chenille blanket and cut two 13"x13" pieces front and back using a paper pattern. (Sew a zig zag edge to prevent any unraveling).

2. TRIM: Pin trim to pillow front, 1/2" in all around and sew down. (Bottom edge of trim faces outer edge of pillow front.)

3. SEW FRONT TO BACK: Pin pillow front to back. Sew around all sides with a 1/2" seam, leaving an opening for pillow form. Trim corners, and turn right side out. Insert pillow form and hand stitch closed.

Dog's Best Friend

What a comfy place for puppy to snooze! Made with four pillow forms, and covered with a classy animal print and coordinated gingham, the entire project can be made in one evening. Pillow forms make up the back and sides; a simple cushy knife-edge form, the bottom. Plumped in a shady corner of the patio, or a secluded nook in your home, this simple-to-make gift of love for your dog or cat will be appreciated more than you'll ever know.

Dog or Cat Bed
(page 99)

You will need:
4 16" square pillow forms
1 1/2 yds. animal print fabric
1/2 yd. green gingham fabric
1/2 yd. oilcloth
1 piece of cardboard 16"x20"
Craft glue

1. Cut animal print fabric - two pieces 21"x27" and one piece 21"x24".

2. Sew three pieces of fabric together along the short ends with the 24" piece in the middle. (1/2" seams).

3. Fold in half lengthwise, right sides together and sew into a tube. Turn right side out.

4. Fold 3 pillow forms in half and sew into cylinders with tight stitches.

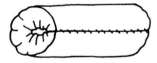

5. Stuff pillow form cylinders one at a time into tube, leaving about 4 inches between them.

6. Tuck the ends of the fabric into the cylinders on each end and glue.

7. Fold into a "U" shape. Tuck raw ends into holes in cylinders. Glue inside to secure.

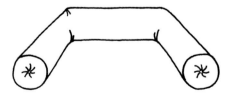

8. Cut cardboard into a 16"x20" piece. Cover with oilcloth or other sturdy, washable fabric. Hot glue to cardboard. (An alternative would be to use a remnant of linoleum or other flooring.)

9. Glue or sew Velcro to the three sides of the cardboard in about one inch.

10. Glue or sew Velcro to the bottom of the bolsters.

11. Cut green gingham fabric 17"x17" and 2 pieces 12"x17".

12. BACK: On wrong side of the two 12"x17" pieces, turn in a 1/2" hem on the long ends, press. Turn in another 1/2", press, pin and machine stitch close to edge. Remove pins. With right side facing up and hemmed edges on the inside, overlap the two back pieces by 5" so that they create one 17"x17" piece. Pin together along hemmed edges.

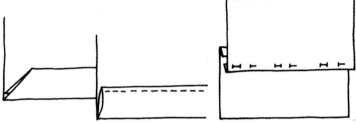

Pin the front to the back, right sides together. Sew a 1/2" seam all around, trim corners, remove pins, turn right side out and insert pillow form.

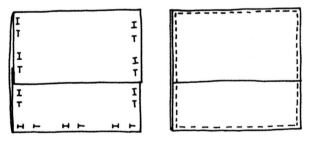

13. Cut two pieces of cardboard in 3" circles and two pieces of animal print fabric in 5" circles. Wrap the fabric around the cardboard and glue. With hot glue gun, glue these pieces to the ends of the bolsters.

General Instructions

As seen in this book, there are endless possibilities when making pillows. Just by selecting different fabrics, shapes, embellishments, and styles, any room can be transformed with the addition of beautiful pillows. Some pillows are easy enough for a child to make and some are a bit more complicated. Whichever one you choose to try, we hope that you'll have fun and that you'll end up with a perfect accent piece for your home. If you choose to make a pillow as a gift, there are several ideas in the Gifts of Love chapter. Perhaps one of these will be the perfect gift you've been looking for. Or one of these ideas will inspire you to try something completely different, designed especially for the person you have in mind. After you select the type of pillow you'd like to make, read the following instructions to get you started.

Where do I start?

First decide where you would like to put the pillow - on a bed, couch, windowseat, etc. From there you can figure out the size, shape, the color, and the type of fabric.

If the pillow is for a gift - what's the occasion, who is it for, what color would they like, what are their interests.

What do I need before I start?

To measure
yardstick
12" ruler
drafting triangle
carpenter's square
tape measure

To mark
dressmaker's chalk
wax pencil
transfer pen
transfer paper

To cut
sharp scissors
embroidery scissors
old scissors for cutting paper
rotary cutter and board
pinking shears

To iron
steam iron
padded ironing board
pressing cloth

To sew
sewing machine
zipper foot
machine needles
hand sewing needles
embroidery needles
safety pins
dressmaker pins
upholstery needle for tufting

Fabrics

Let your imagination go when selecting fabrics. This is the fun part of creating unique pillows. You can be guided according to your present furnishings and accessories in regards to color, trim, and special embellishments.

For pillows that will receive heavy use choose a firm, woven fabric that will keep its shape.

For decorative pillows choose loose weaves for texture and interest.

For durability select firm woven, synthetics or blends that will last longer.

For outdoor cushions you'll want fade resistant (light colored, solids are most fade resistant), easy care fabrics.

Natural fabrics (cotton, linen, silk, wool) - are easy to work with, comfortable, feel good, wear well and retain their shape. But they will shrink, wrinkle and fade.

Synthetic (acetate, acrylic, nylon, polyester, rayon) are durable, easy care, washable, retain shape, and are wrinkle-free. But they're not as easy to handle and can be uncomfortable.

A good choice is a cotton and polyester blend which has the qualities of both fibers.

Selecting Fabrics for Pillows

Make up a notebook with a section for each room of your house. Include paint chips, fabric swatches of your furniture, drapes, and curtains. Add measurements of furniture. And don't forget to add lots of pictures from magazines and books for inspiration.

Shop at fabric stores, fabric departments of discount chains, upholstery shops. Look for vintage fabrics and accessories at flea markets, auctions, antique shops or garage sales.

More Fabric Facts

Choose fabrics with a straight grain (cross-wise threads running perpendicular to lengthwise threads). Don't use printed fabric that is off-grain or the pillow will be crooked.

Tip -
Buy a pillow pattern and keep it in your decorating notebook. This will give fabric requirements for several different types and sizes of pillows. It's well worth the investment and will keep you from having to do the math for each individual pillow that you make. (Buy a pattern when there's a big sale or when the fabric stores are selling old stock.)

How much fabric to buy

A. Knife edge - enough for top and bottom (add enough all around for the 1/2" seams.)

B. Bolster - enough to encircle round form and for end pieces. Top and bottom pieces should be cut exact size of the form, adding 1/4" to zipper edges if planned.

After making your calculations, add several inches of fabric just to make sure you have enough. If you are using a fabric with a large pattern, be sure to purchase enough so that the pattern will center on the pillow correctly.

To Press

To get a great looking pillow, you must press or iron as you sew. Seams that are pressed as you're making your pillow will make the fabric lay better and give a more finished appearance. Always use a pressing cloth as you're ironing to protect your fabric. Press the wrong side of the fabric. Start with a low temperature until you know how hot you can go with the fabric you're ironing. It also helps to use spray starch to keep seams flat and make joints smooth.

Thread

Polyester - for synthetic fabrics

Cotton wrapped - for natural fibers

Whether polyester or cotton - use a thread that is slightly darker than the fabric or one that matches the main color of a print fabric.

Pillow Forms

All the pillows in this book were made using ready-made pillow forms.

Pillow forms come in a variety of shapes and sizes. But there will be times when you'll want to make a pillow with a different shape - such as a star or heart. In this case, you'll need to make your own pillow form.

Making your own pillow form

You can make one using muslin or a plain fabric for a covering. Cut and sew the pillow form in the desired shape leaving an opening for filling. Stuff with either cotton batting or loose stuffing to the preferred plumpness. Hand stitch the opening closed.

(Remember to cut your pillow form fabric slightly smaller than your finished pillow).

To make a smooth pillow -

Take a fist size wad of filling and gently pull it apart to fluff and separate the fibers. Use a crochet hook or chop stick to stuff filling into the corners. Or wrap a layer of batting around a pillow form and insert in the pillow.

For box pillows -

Use Polyurethane foam which comes in sheets and pre-cut forms. To soften a foam form, wrap with batting.

Other fillings for pillow forms:

Kapok - decorators and upholsterers prefer kapok - which fills pillows softly and completely.

Down - the ultimate filling. However it's expensive and hard to handle. If you really want to have a pillow form of down - have an upholsterer make one for you.

Tip -
When purchasing pillow forms - take tape measure with you to the store and measure the form as they are sometimes 1 or 2 inches larger than the label says.

Welt

Welt is also called welting or piping. It's an edge for a pillow, cushion or bolster. A welt can be made or purchased. Purchased welt comes either packaged or by the yard.

To make your own welt, you will need:

1. For a knife edge pillow -
the perimeter plus 3 inches for joining ends.

2. For a boxed cushion -
double the perimeter and add 6 inches.

3. For a bolster pillow -
double the end perimeter plus 6 inches

You'll also need "cable cord" which comes in various diameters. Usually you will use 1/4" thick cord.

Use a bias cut casing of fabric to cover the cord. This ensures that the welt will fit smoothly around the curves and corners of the pillow.

Make the bias casing wide enough to wrap around the cord with enough extra for twice the width of the seam allowance.

If you're making one or two pillows, you'll need to cut and piece bias strips.

First establish the bias line by folding corner of the fabric so that the selvage aligns with the crosswise cut; then press the fold and cut along the fold.

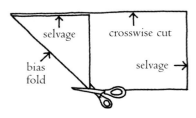

Then use the diagonal cut as a guideline and measure and mark 1 5/8" wide strips parallel to the cut. Stop when bottom edge of strip is no longer on crosswise cut. Cut along lines.

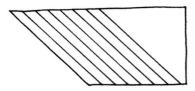

With right sides together place two strips at a right angle, offset slightly and join with a 1/4" seam; press seam open. Sew all strips to make one continuous strip.

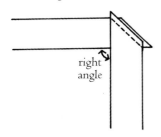

Lay cord along the center of wrong side of bias casing. Fold casing over cord and align raw edges.

Using longest stitch on sewing machine, and zipper foot - sew through casing close to cord. Don't crowd casing because you'll want to stitch pillow seams between welt stitching and cord.

Stretch bias casing as you sew to help welt lie smoothly in the pillow seams.

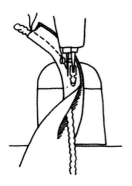

Gathered welt

To make a gathered welt ("ruching"), stitch the empty casing and thread the cord through and gather the casing. Use light or medium weight fabric for the gathered welt. An average bias casing is 1 5/8" wide and the cord 1/4" thick. The casing should be 2 to 4 times the length of the cord.

You will prepare the bias casing according to the instructions on page 104.

Fold the bias casing lengthwise, wrong sides together and raw edges aligned. Set machine on longest stitch and baste casing 3/8" from raw edges.

Tape one edge to prevent fraying. Attach a safety pin at taped edge and thread through the empty casing gathering evenly. Pin the other end of cord as it reaches end of casing to keep it from pulling through.

When machine basting welt to top pillow piece, sew on welt stitching; when sewing pillow pieces together, stitch seam between welt stitching and cord.

To install a zipper, press under 3/4" seam allowance on both edges where zipper will go; when basting welt along zipper edge position welt stitching over the crease.

Begin at the middle of either edge except zipper edge, lay welt on right side of top pillow piece, welt seam allowances aligned with raw edges of pillow piece.

Set machine at longest stitch and use zipper foot. Baste 1 1/2" from end of welt.

Stitch welt to within 1 1/2" of corner. Make 3 diagonal cuts into welt seam to turn corners easily.

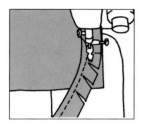

Gently curve around corner. Leave needle in fabric, raise foot, pivot fabric and welt, lower foot and stitch down side. Continue stitching along sides and around corners.

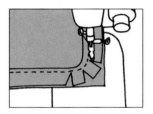

Continue sewing around pillow to within 1 1/2" of first welt end. Stop stitching, leave needle in fabric. Cut off second welt end so it will overlap first end by one inch. Take out last inch of stitches from welt casing on second end; pull out and cut off one inch of cord.

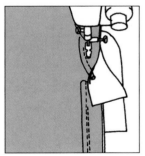

On the same end, fold casing under 3/8"; lap it around first end. Slip welt back into seam and hold in place and finish stitching welt to pillow piece.

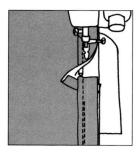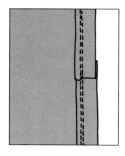

To cross ends, sew around pillow to one inch of first welt end. Stop stitching, leave needle in fabric. Cut off welt so it overlaps first welt end by 1 1/2 inches. Pull out and cut off 3/4 inch of cord from each welt end. With both ends extending into seam allowance, cross empty casing and finish stitching welt to pillow pieces.

Pillow Closures

There are several ways to close a pillow. The choice is dependent on the type of pillow and how much use it will receive.

If you don't plan to wash the pillow, you can close the seam with hand stitching after the pillow form is inserted.

Another way to close a pillow is with an overlap closure. This is an easier method than adding a zipper and you'll still be able to remove the pillow form for laundering. Adding a velcro strip to the overlap creates a neat, secure closure.

Zippers

Most pillows don't require a zipper - only those that will be removed often for cleaning.

There are three types of zippers:
1. Centered
2. Lapped in plain seam
3. Lapped in welted seam

Zippers are available in two ways:
1. Packaged (in varying lengths)
2. On a roll - sold by the inch

If buying a zipper by the inch - buy it one inch longer than the opening. Then handstitch the teeth 1/2 inch from bottom to make a zipper stop.

Tip -
To hold zipper in position, Use a glue stick to secure a zipper to the seam allowances. The glue should be applied to both edges of the right side of the zipper tape and pressed in position on the seam allowances, right side down.

Or use double-faced tape for holding zippers in position. The tape strip can be placed on the right side of the zipper tape, close to the teeth.

106

Centered zipper
(for square, rectangular or boxed pillows)

This type of zipper should be centered in the back boxing strip and should be equal to the finished length of the pillow's back edge plus 3 inches.

For a round boxed cushion the zipper should be a third of the finished circumference.

1. Fold back boxing strip in half lengthwise, right sides together and press fold

2. Stitch and back stitch along folded edge using 3/4" seam allowance for first and last 3/4"

Then using longest stitch setting - baste the length of zipper opening.

Cut along fold and press seam open.

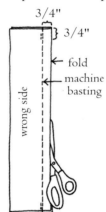

3. Attach zipper foot to machine. Place boxing strip to left and extend the right-hand seam.

Open zipper.

Lay one side face down on extended seam allowance so teeth are against center seam.

Machine baste the length of zipper through the zipper tape and seam allowance only - stitch 1/4" from teeth.

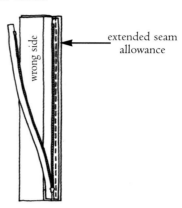

4. Open boxing strip, close zipper and smooth it over pressed seam. Pin or baste unstitched zipper tape through all thicknesses.

Set machine to regular length stitch. Start at the top next to zipper tab and stitch zipper tape 1/4 inch from teeth.

Stitch across zipper below stop, up the other side and across top. Backstitch at beginning and end. Remove center basting; open zipper several times.

Lapped zipper in pillow bottom or unwelted edge
(for knife edge or bolster pillows)

Zipper should be 2 to 3 inches shorter than the finished length of the pillow edge.

For a 36" bolster - use a zipper sold by the inch or use two shorter zippers so the tabs meet at the middle of the lengthwise seam.

1. Prepare zipper seam
Zipper should be centered lengthwise in seam. Subtract length of zipper from cut length of seam edge; divide remainder by 2 to determine length of short seams above and below zipper opening.

For instance:
knife edge 14" square
cut size 15" x 15"
zipper - 12"
short seams above and below opening - 1 1/2 inches long
(15-12 divided by 2 = 1 1/2)
With right sides facing and raw edges even, pin edges where zipper will go. Stitch and backstitch short seams above and below zipper opening. Machine baste length of zipper opening and press seam open.

2. Baste Zipper
Attach zipper foot. With pillow pieces (right sides together) on the left and one seam allowance extended (top pillow piece underneath if zipper is going in edge), lay one side of open zipper face down on extended seam allowance, with teeth on center seam line; zipper tab and stop should be at points where basting begins and ends. Machine baste 1/4" from teeth the length of zipper through zipper tape and seam allowance only.

3. Stitch Zipper
Shift zipper foot to other side of needle. Close zipper and turn face up, smoothing fabric away from zipper. Set machine to regular length and sew along narrow fold between center seam and zipper teeth. Open pillow pieces, turn zipper face down and pin or baste unstitched zipper tape through all thicknesses. On right or wrong side, 1/4" from zipper teeth stitch across zipper below stop, up the side, across top. Back stitch at beginning and end. If stitching from right side, check to make sure stitches catch zipper tape.

On a bolster, you will be stitching inside tube when you stitch zipper. Shift fabric at opening to expose zipper as you stitch down its length. Remove basting; open zipper several inches.

Lapped zipper in welted edge
Use a zipper 2 to 3 inches shorter than the finished length of the pillow edge. If the zipper is basted and stitched carefully, the teeth will be concealed beneath the welt.

1. Prepare Zipper Seam
See step #1 for "lapped zipper in pillow or unwelted edge".

Fold out creased edge on bottom pieces. With right sides together, pin top and bottom pieces along edge where zipper will go. Stitch and backstitch above and below zipper opening, using 3/4" seam allowance.

2. Stitch Zipper
With right sides together (welted piece underneath) pull back top piece to expose seam allowance below. Lay one side at open zipper face down on extended seam allowance, zipper tab at top of opening and zipper teeth on top of welt. Pin and stitch close to teeth the length of zipper tape, stitching through zipper tape, welt seam allowances, and pillow seam allowances only. Open pieces so right sides are up. Zipper is attached on one side, below welt. close zipper and lay creased edge over teeth. Pin or baste through all thicknesses. On right or wrong side, 1/4 inch from zipper teeth, stitch across zipper at bottom, up the side, and across top. Backstitch at beginning and end. If stitching from right side, check to be sure that stitches catch zipper tape. Remove basting; open zipper several inches.

Transferring Patterns

Method 1 - Using Transfer Paper
Use dark colored paper for light colored fabrics and light colored paper for dark colored fabrics.   Trace desired pattern from the book. Position design (pattern) on the fabric. Pin or hold in place along one edge. Place transfer paper (chalk side down) between pattern and fabric. Use a dull pencil or stylus to draw over lines of pattern. Remove pattern and transfer paper.

Method 2 - Hot Iron Transfer Pencil
Use pencil to draw over lines of pattern on back of tracing paper. Position pattern, transfer pencil side down, on fabric. Pin in place. Following manufacturer's instructions, transfer design to fabric. Remove pattern.

Making Photo Iron-on Transfers

An excellent product for transferring photos to fabric is Photo Effects by Hues, Inc. The transfer paper is available for use with either copy machines or computer printers.

Copy your photo onto the transfer paper (this can be done by most print shops) in color or black and white. The transfer can then be applied to fabric with either a household iron or a heat press.

Follow manufacturer's instructions for using transfer paper with computer printers.

Care instructions: Turn item inside out (if possible). Machine or hand wash with mild soap in cool water. Do not use bleach, fabric softener or hot water. Tumble dry on low and remove promptly.

Tea Dyeing

To achieve an antique or old-fashioned look to new fabric, soak in a solution of brewed tea. Place about 10 tea bags in a pot. Fill with boiling water and let steep about 10 minutes. Soak fabric in the tea, using a wooden spoon to dip and stir. Soak for several minutes. Remove from tea and wring out gently. Allow to dry and then press.

For a darker, antique look - soak fabric in a solution of coffee. Add two tablespoons of instant coffee to two cups of hot water. Soak for several minutes. Allow to dry and then press.

Using Fusible Webbing

1. Trace applique shape onto paper side (smooth side) of the fusible web. Cut out, leaving a small amount of paper beyond the shape.

2. Place fusible web (rough side) onto wrong side of the fabric. Iron over the paper.

3. Cut out traced shape and fabric.

4. Peel off the paper, place the shape on the background fabric and fuse according to manufacturer's instructions.

5. For items that will be laundered, pre-wash fabric to remove sizing. Sizing may keep fabrics from fusing.

6. Always pre-test to make sure iron is not overheated. Overheating may melt the adhesive through the fabric.

Heat Setting

After painting onto fabric, the project should be heat set to make the design permanent.

Let paint dry completely.   Set iron to cotton setting.   Press on wrong side of fabric (using a pressing cloth) for about 60 seconds.

Folded Ribbon Rose

1. Roll one end of ribbon tightly five or six times to form a compact tube (A).

2. Take a few stitches at the base (B).

3. Fold the ribbon diagonally (C).

4. Roll this tube onto the folded ribbon and stitch (D).

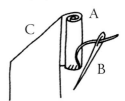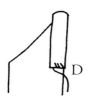

5. Hold the rose at the base and loosely roll the top to the end of the fold and stitch (E).

6. Continue to fold and roll, forming petals (F). When the rose is full enough, trim away any excess. Fold ends under and sew to base.

Hand Stitching

Whipstitch

A fast, strong stitch for closing the openings of a pillow. To whipstitch - make overcasting stitches about 1/4" apart.

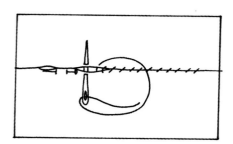

Blindstitch

For invisible closures on solid-color fabrics. For blindstitching, use small, evenly spaced stitches.

Slightly fold back the creased edges of opening. Working from right to left, take a tiny stitch along one side of one fold. Take the next stitch opposite folded edge, a little ahead of the first. Work back and forth, making sure stitches are close and evenly spaced. About every six stitches, pull thread tight, but not so tight that fabric wrinkles. Secure with a few stitches at the end of the opening.

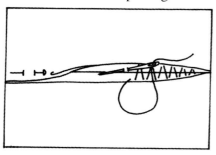

Blanket Stitch

1. Come up at A. Circle the floss counter-clockwise. Hold it down with left thumb.

2. Go down at B, up at C (close to A).

3. With floss under the point of needle, pull through.

4. Go down at D, up at E, etc.

Single Feather Stitch

1. Come up at A. Circle yarn counterclockwise. Hold it down with left thumb.

2. Go down at B, up at C (on same line as A) and with floss under point of needle, pull through.

3. Circle yarn counterclockwise.

4. Go down at D, up at E, and with floss under point of needle, pull through, and continue.

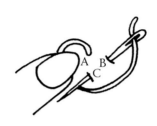 

Silk Ribbon Embroidery

Cut ribbon into 12" lengths. You may wish to press it (using low heat) to remove any creases.

Needles:

You will need a #24 embroidery (chenille) needle.

Threading and locking:

Thread ribbon through eye of needle. Pull through about 3" and then pierce the end of the ribbon (that you've just pulled through) with the needle (about 1/4" from the end.) Pull back on the opposite end of the ribbon until it locks around the eye of the needle.

Knotting the end of the ribbon:

Hold the end of the ribbon and form a circle with the end of the ribbon and the point of the needle. Fold the end of the ribbon down (as shown) and push the needle through the two layers of ribbon. Pull the ribbon through to form a knot.

Ending stitches:

Run needle under the backs of several stitches.

Handling the ribbon:

Usually you'll want to keep the ribbon flat, smooth and loose. Use the thumb of your opposite hand to keep the ribbon flat as you stitch.

Transferring design to fabric:

Hold the fabric against a window (in sunlight) with your pattern behind it. Trace very lightly with a pencil. Be sure to cover all pencil lines when stitching. You may wish to just use dots for placement of stitches.

Refer to the photograph often as you work.

Silk Ribbon Embroidery Stitches

Japanese Ribbon Stitch

1. Bring the needle up at A. Lay the ribbon flat on the fabric and push the needle back through the ribbon at B. Gently and loosely pull the needle through to the back. The ribbon will curl at the tip.

Lazy Daisy

1. Bring needle up at A. Keep ribbon flat, untwisted and full.

2. Push needle down through fabric at B. and back up at C. passing the ribbon under the needle.

3. Pull the ribbon through, leaving the loop loose and full.

4. Push the needle through on the other side of the ribbon at D.

Spider Web Rose

1. Thread needle with 2 strands of floss.

2. Work straight stitches to form five spokes.

3. Thread the needle with ribbon and bring it up through the fabric at the center of the spokes.

4. Weave the ribbon over one spoke and under the next. Allow the ribbon to twist and keep it loose. Keep going until the spokes are covered.

French Knots

1. Bring the needle up at A.

2. Smoothly wrap ribbon around the needle as many times as desired.

3. Hold ribbon securely off to one side and push needle down through fabric right next to starting point at B. Pull tightly for small French knots, very loosely for larger French knots.

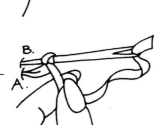

Dainty Floral Bouquet
Tracing Pattern

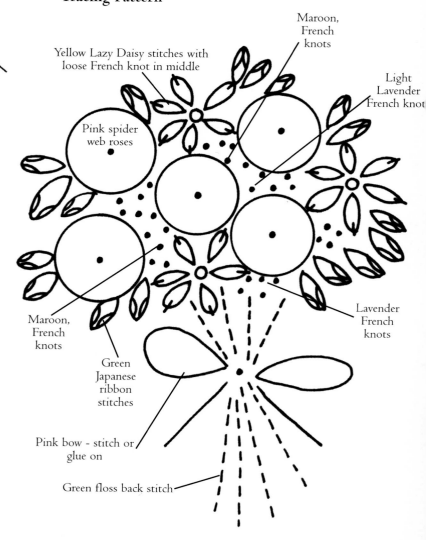

Maroon, French knots

Light Lavender French knot

Yellow Lazy Daisy stitches with loose French knot in middle

Pink spider web roses

Lavender French knots

Maroon, French knots

Green Japanese ribbon stitches

Pink bow - stitch or glue on

Green floss back stitch

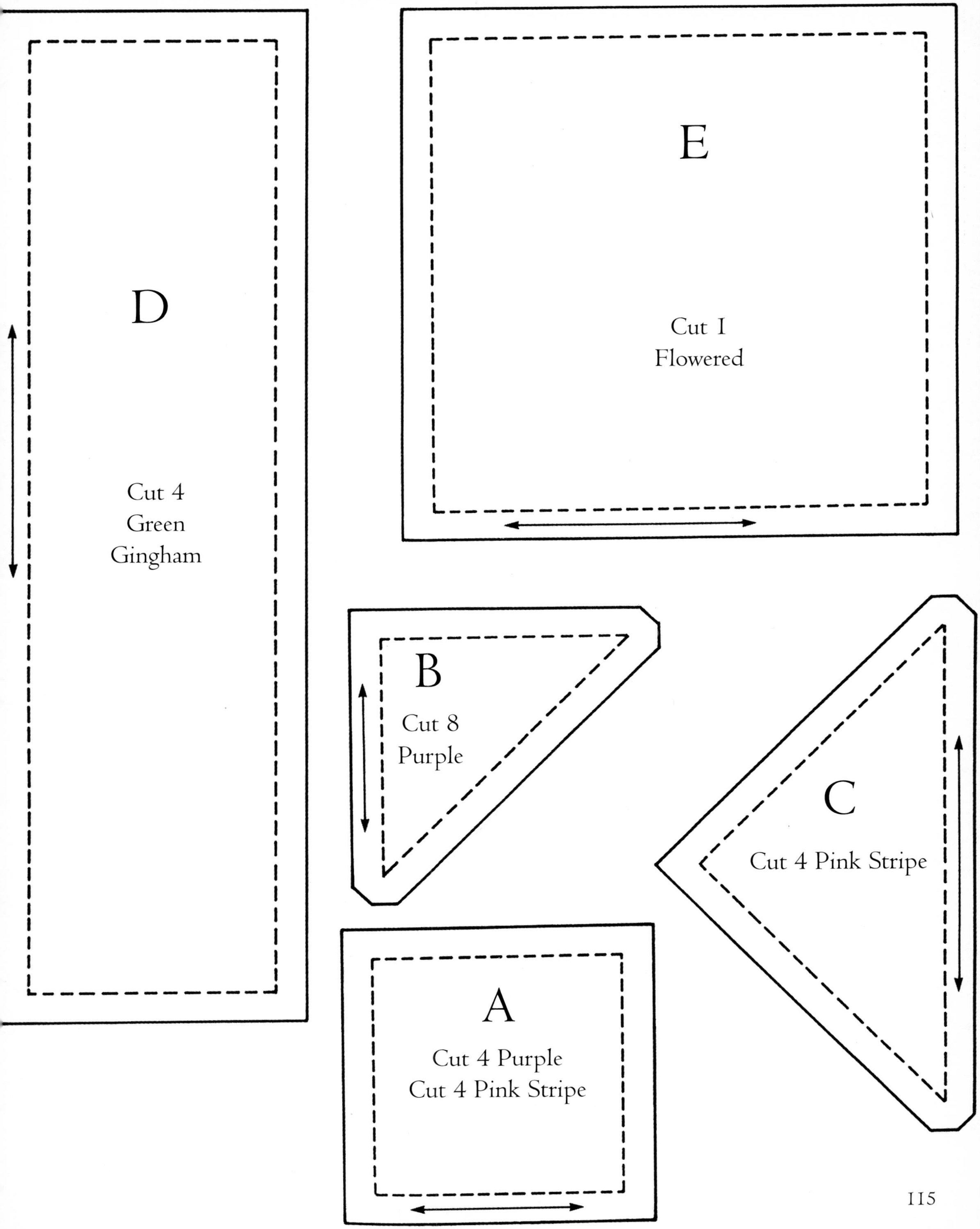

D

Cut 4
Green
Gingham

E

Cut 1
Flowered

B

Cut 8
Purple

C

Cut 4 Pink Stripe

A

Cut 4 Purple
Cut 4 Pink Stripe

Enlarge 200%

Enlarge 200%

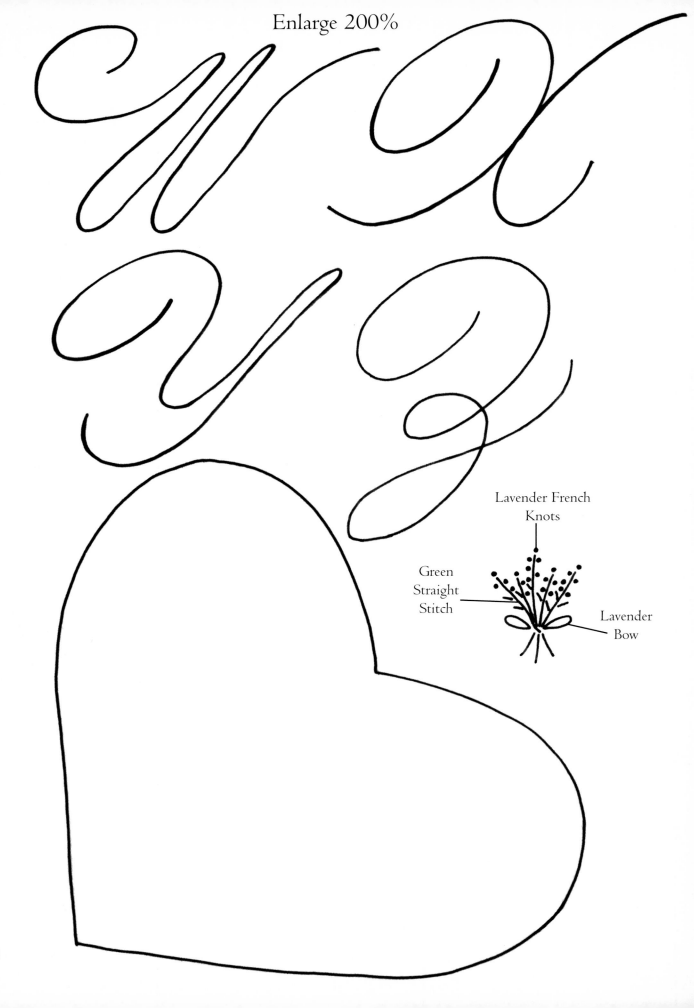

Lavender French
Knots

Green
Straight
Stitch

Lavender
Bow

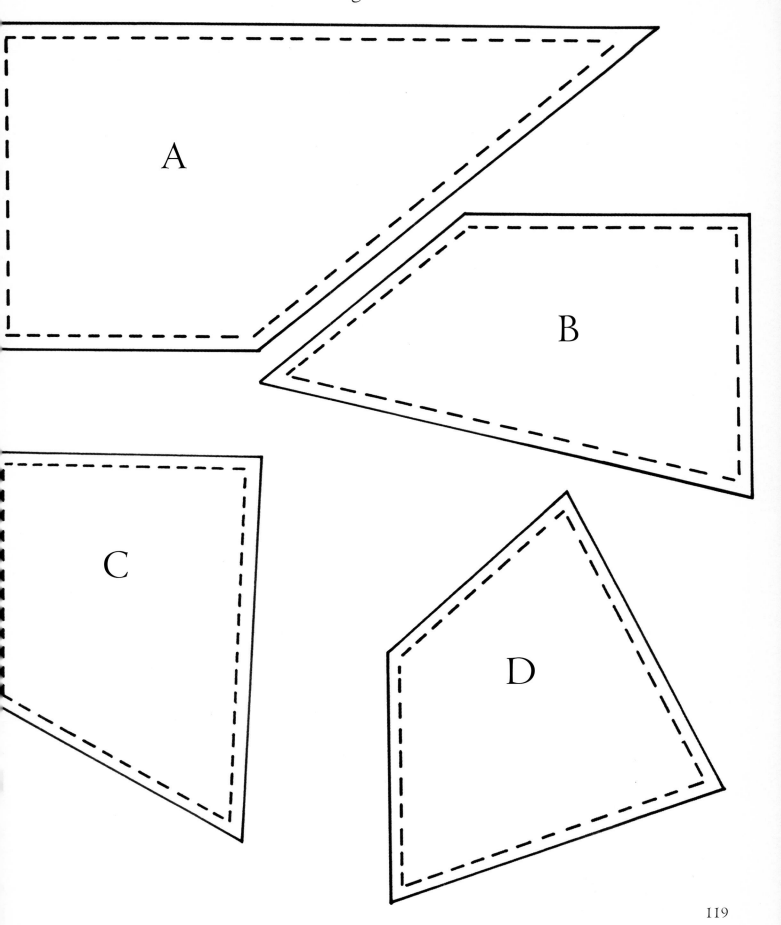

A

B

C

D

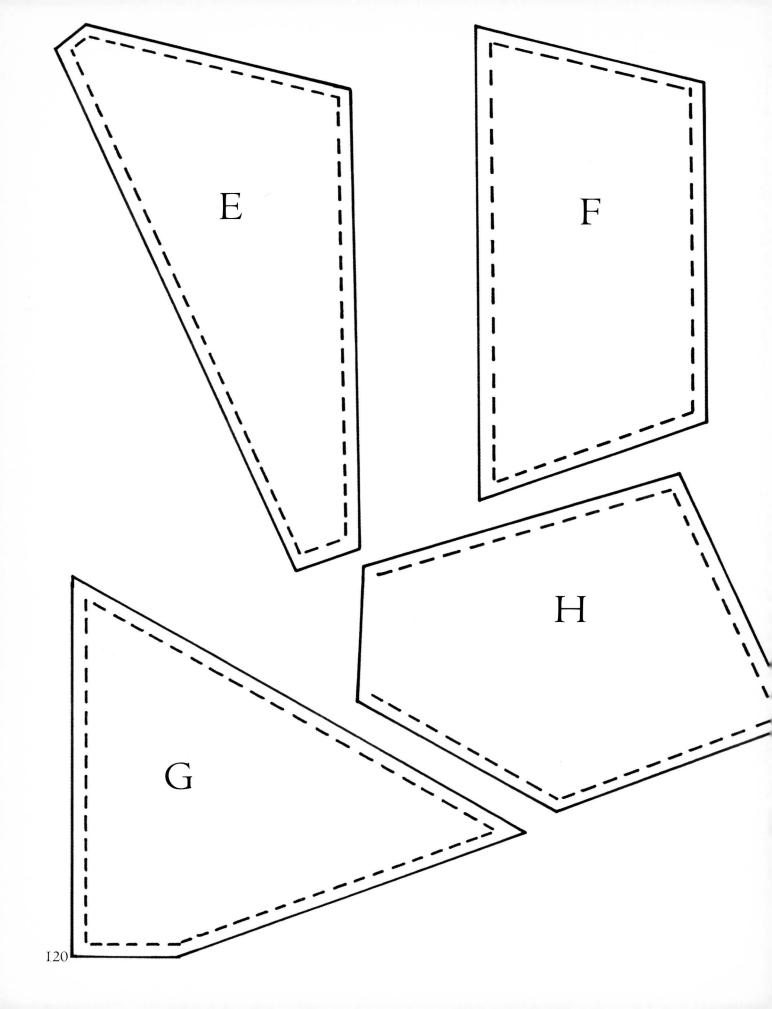

E

F

H

G

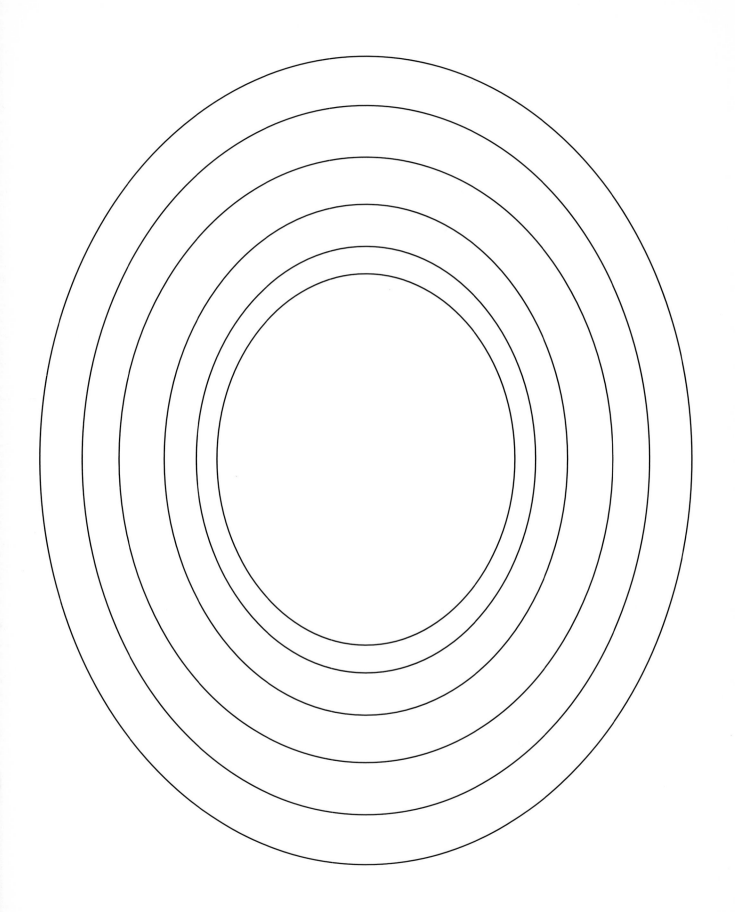

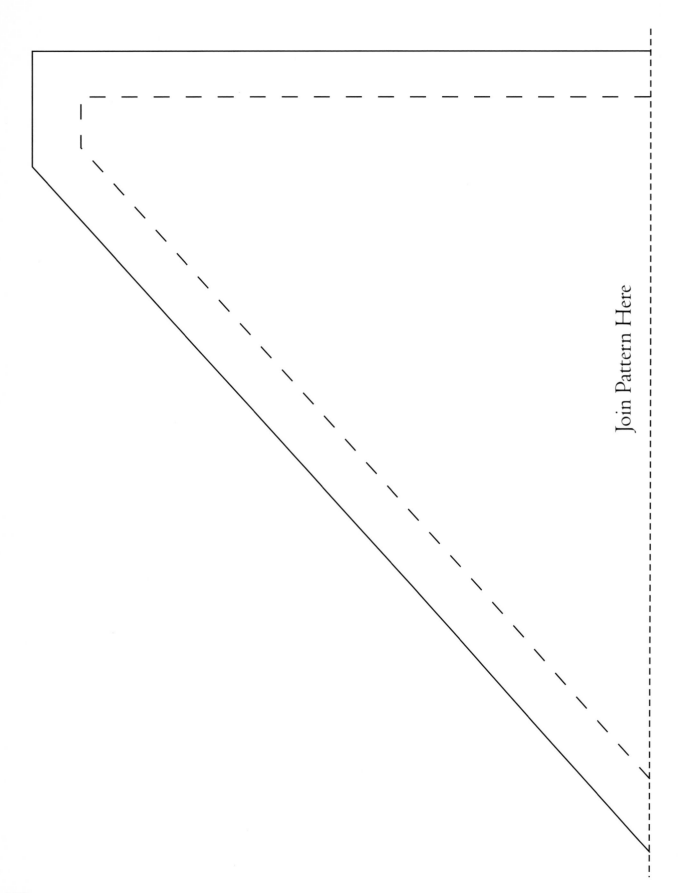

Join Pattern Here

Join Pattern Here

Source List

Silk pillows, silk cord
Arty's
Sinoart, Inc.
Box 1650
Windsor, Ca 95492

Trims, Tassels, Cords
Conso
513 N. Duncan Bypass
Union, SC 29379

Paint
Delta Technical Coatings
2550 Pellissier Pl.
Whittier, Ca 90601

Pillow Forms
Fairfield Processing
88 Rose Hill Ave.
Danbury, Ct 06810

Paint Brushes
Loew Cornell
563 Chestnut Ave.
Teaneck, NJ 07666

Linen Fabric
MCG Textiles
13845 Magnolia Ave.
Chino, Ca 91710

Ribbon
C.M. Offray
360 Rt. 24
Chester, NJ 07930

Fabric
P&B Textiles
1580 Gilbreth Rd.
Burlingame, Ca 94010

Ribbon
Ribbon Connections
(exclusive distributors of silk satin ribbon)
4971 Teagarden
San Leandro, Ca 94577

Rubber Stamps
Rubber Stampede
P.O. Box 246
Berkeley, Ca 94701

Fabric
Waverly
79 Madison Ave.
New York, NY 10016

We would also like to thank the following people for their extra-special cooperation on this book: Donna Wilder of Fairfield Processing, Pam Pugh of Conso Trims, Catherine Horton of Offray Ribbons and Tim Noder of Waverly Fabrics.

Index

Figures in bold refer to photographs

Acknowledgements

The designers listed below contributed the following projects for this book:

Decorator Style
Faux Leopard Pair, 5
Joni Prittie
Toile Cameo, 7
Joni Prittie
Red Toile Envelope, 9
Holly Witt
Toile Flange, 9
Becky King
Gathered Tapestry Roses, 9
Becky King
Golden Medallions, 13
Joni Prittie
Silk Floral, 14
Barbara Finwall
Ethereal Pockets, 15
Barbara Finwall

Fresh Country Style
Ruffled Gingham and Morning
Glories, 19
Barbara Finwall
French Provencal, 21
Holly Witt
Bow Tied Country, 22
Becky King
Scotty, 23
Holly Witt
Organza Shadow, 25
Holly Witt
All Tied Up in Ribbons
Floral Ribbon Rose, 29
Karen Cunagin
Dainty Floral Bouquet, 31
Barbara Finwall
Feathered Friend, 33
Karen Cunagin
Woven Stripes, 35
Karen Cunagin
Ribbon Framed Rose, 36
Becky King

Ribbon Loops, 37
Joni Prittie

Just for the Fun of It
Bows of Silk, 40
Joni Prittie
Felt Roses, 41
Holly Witt
Buttons Galore, 43
Holly Witt
A Rose is a Rose, 44
Holly Witt
Cherries Jubille, 45
Holly Witt
Magical Leaves, 47
Holly Witt
Patchwork
Floral Nine-Patch, 51
Holly Witt
Patchwork Star, 53
Holly Witt
Victorian Crazy Quilt, 54
Holly Witt
Silken Stripes, 55
Barbara Finwall

The Male Room
Dad's Ties, 58
Holly Witt
Reading Pillow, 59
Judy Aafedt
Natural Wonders, 61
Holly Witt
Heartfelt, 62
Holly Witt
Appliqued Memories, 63
Karen Cunagin

Sew Easy
All designs in Sew Easy Chapter
are by Judy Aafedt

Bits and Pieces of Old
Buttons and Lace, 79
Holly Witt

Vintage Fabrications, 81
Karen Cunagin
Unfinished Symphony, 83
Karen Cunagin
Memory Patches, 84
Barbara Finwall
God Bless America, 85
Becky King
Lacy Velvet Neckroll, 86
Karen Cunagin
Folk Art Sampler, 87
Barbara Finwall

Gifts of Love
Family Album, 90
Holly Witt
Portrait Pillows, 91
Holly Witt
Lavender & Lace, 93
Holly Witt
Wedding Memories, 95
Holly Witt
Alternative Bulletin Board, 96
Holly Witt
Sleepy Time Pillows, 97
Holly Witt
Dog's Best Friend, 99
Judy Aafedt

We would like to thank Presley Homes for allowing us to photograph in their beautiful model homes in Fallbrook, Calif.

A special thanks to our animal models Brandy (page 99), Tippi (page 79), and Chloe, our cover girl who also appears on page 25.

Grateful acknowledgment is made to Sunset Books for permission to reprint instructions from their book How To Make Pillows, copyright 1980©, Lane Publishing Co.